Into the Fire

AFRICAN AMERICANS
SINCE 1970

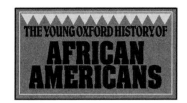

Robin D. G. Kelley and Earl Lewis
General Editors

Into the Fire

◇ ◇ ◇

AFRICAN AMERICANS
SINCE 1970

ROBIN D. G. KELLEY

Oxford University Press
New York • Oxford

Elleza
This one's for you!
Love, Daddy

Oxford University Press

Oxford New York
Athens Auckland Bangkok Bombay
Calcutta Cape Town Dar es Salaam Delhi
Florence Hong Kong Istanbul Karachi
Kuala Lumpur Madras Madrid Melbourne
Mexico City Nairobi Paris Singapore
Taipei Tokyo Toronto
and associated companies in

Berlin Ibadan

Published by Oxford University Press, Inc.,
198 Madison Avenue, New York, New York 10016

Design: Sandy Kaufman
Layout: Leonard Levitsky
Picture research: Lisa Kirchner, Laura Kreiss

Library of Congress Cataloging in Publication Data
Kelley, Robin D. G.
Into the fire : African Americans since 1970 / by Robin D. G. Kelley
p.   cm. — (Young Oxford history of African Americans ; vol. 10)
Includes bibliographical references and index.
ISBN 0-19-508701-1 (library ed.); ISBN 0-19-508502-7 (series, library ed.)
1. Afro-Americans—History—1964- —Juvenile literature.
I. Title. II. Series: Young Oxford history of African Americans : vol. 10
E185.615.K37   1995
973'.0496073—dc20   95-6627
CIP

3 5 7 9 8 6 4 2

Printed in the United States of America
on acid-free paper

On the cover: Fabrics of 125th Street, collage by Allen Stringfellow
Frontispiece: Three black men salvage what remains of a burned-down building in Newark, New Jersey, on a cold November day in 1989.
Page 9: Detail from *The Contribution of the Negro to Democracy in America*, (1943) by Charles White, 11'9" x 17'3"
Hampton University Museum, Hampton, Virginia.

CONTENTS

◇ ◇ ◇

ROBIN D.G. KELLEY
EARL LEWIS

INTRODUCTION

When a situation went from bad to worse, elders would sometimes say it "fell out of the frying pan and into the fire." This timeless phrase succinctly captures what has happened to the majority of African Americans since the 1970s. Of course, when the 1960s came to a close most black people were surprisingly optimistic. The civil rights movement had made remarkable gains, and many people believed that the black power movement might achieve for African Americans the self-determination they had been seeking for the past three centuries. And there were some stunning victories, especially in the arena of electoral politics. Several major cities elected black mayors, African-American representation in Congress increased significantly, and a black man named Jesse Jackson actually became a serious contender for the Presidency. As corporate board rooms became slightly more integrated and black college-educated professionals moved to newly built suburban homes, the black middle class expanded. Thus a handful of African Americans escaped the frying pan altogether.

The majority were not so lucky. The period after 1970 was marked by economic changes that had negative effects on black workers: the disappearance of heavy industry, the flight of American industry to foreign lands, and the loss of jobs for millions of workers across the country. Permanent unemployment and underemployment became a way of life for many. Only a few years after Lyndon Johnson's War on Poverty had been declared a victory in the late 1960s, the number of black poor began to grow dramatically. And despite the increased presence of

Black-on-black violence, along with poverty, joblessness, crime, and racial discrimination, has been one of the most pressing issues facing black urban communities since 1970. This poster, pasted on a Detroit storefront in 1993, publicizes a play about the rising homicide rate among young black men.

African Americans in political office, city services declined, federal spending on cities dried up, affirmative action programs were dismantled, blatant acts of racism began to rise again, and the United States entered a deep economic recession.

Economic decline, poverty, and rising racism in the "post-segregation" age is only part of the story. This volume also tells the story of how an increasingly diverse and always complicated black community resisted oppression; struggled for power; dealt with internal tensions, conflicts, and differences; and profoundly shaped American culture. It examines, among other things, the rebirth of black nationalism; the rise of a new black conservative movement (called neo-conservatism); the challenge of black feminism; the impact of Caribbean immigration on African-American communities; the increase of interethnic tensions; and the roots of rap music and hip-hop culture.

Unlike most other history books, parts of *Into the Fire* might be recognizable to many young readers. After all, they have lived through many of these events, some of which have become part of their memories. Yet, there are many things contained in these pages that will not be familiar at all, for this book attempts to weave together our public memory with stories that have been hidden from view. It is the kind of book that will challenge and be challenged by readers of all ages. And we hope that it will convince young people that they have the power to determine the outcome of chapters yet to be written.

This book is part of an 11-volume series that narrates African-American history from the 15th through the 20th centuries. Since the 1960s, a rapid explosion in research on black Americans has significantly modified previous understanding of that experience. Studies of slavery, African-American culture, social protest, families, and religion, for example, silenced those who had previously labeled black Americans insignificant historical actors. This new research followed a general upsurge of interest in the social and cultural experiences of the supposedly powerless men and women who did not control the visible reins of power. The result has been a careful and illuminating portrait of how ordinary people make history and serve as the architects of their own destinies.

This series explores many aspects of the lives of African Americans. It describes how blacks shaped and changed the history of this nation. It also places the lives of African Americans in the context of the Americas as a whole. We start the story more than a century before the day in 1619 when 19 "negars" stepped off a Spanish ship in Jamestown, Virginia, and end with the relationship between West Indian immigrants and African Americans in large urban centers like New York in the late 20th century.

At the same time, the series addresses a number of interrelated questions: What was life like for the first Africans to land in the Americas, and what were the implications for future African Americans? Were all Africans and African Americans enslaved? How did race shape slavery and how did slavery influence racism? The series also considers questions about male-female relationships, the forging of African-American communities, religious beliefs and practices, the experiences of the young, and the changing nature of social protest. The key events in American history are here, too, but viewed from the perspective of African Americans. The result is a fascinating and compelling story of nearly five centuries of African-American history.

THE YOUNG OXFORD HISTORY OF
AFRICAN AMERICANS

CHAPTER 1

THE REVOLUTION CONTINUES

◇ ◇ ◇

A nyone strolling through the black ghettos of Chicago, Newark, or Los Angeles in 1973 probably noticed posters advertising Oscar Williams's new film, *Five on the Black Hand Side*, pasted along the sides of temporary plywood walls or on abandoned buildings. You could tell by the poster's cartoon illustrations that this was a comedy. In the center is a conservatively dressed black businessman surrounded by dozens of crazy-looking people: some are protesting, some are fighting, some are simply enjoying each other's company. Even though the characters in the poster are decked out in bell bottoms, platform shoes, and serious Afro puffs, this film is not another action-packed ghetto drama about pimps, hipsters, and black crime-fighters, like the ever-popular *Superfly* or *Shaft*. Instead it is a comedy about the trials and tribulations of the black middle class. Challenging the more common films about hustlers and ghetto violence, the text of the poster summons us all to the theater: "You've been coffy-tized, blacula-rized and super-flied—but now you're gonna be glorified, unified and filled-with-pride . . . when you see *Five On the Black Hand Side*."

The poster, like the film itself, marked a transition taking place in black political attitudes. During the early to mid-1970s, there was a little less talk of revolution and more emphasis on winning local elections. The push for black pride and black unity we often associate with the "sixties generation" did not die, however. On the contrary, the ideas of the

Despite their use of stereotypical characters such as pimps, hustlers, radical protesters, corrupt politicians, and racist cops, black action films in the 1970s reflected the conflicts and political issues facing African Americans during the post–civil rights era. Many of these issues are hinted at in this poster for Five on the Black Hand Side, *a 1973 film directed by Oscar Williams.*

"black power" movement reached its apex in the 1970s. Black was in. Afros and African garments were not only in style but had become even more popular among ordinary African Americans. The slogan "Black is Beautiful" lingered well after the decline of black power. Militant black nationalist organizations, such as the Black Panther party, the Republic of New Afrika, and the Black Liberation Front, continued to gain local support in urban neighborhoods for their advocacy of armed self-defense, black control over political and economic institutions, and efforts to build black pride and self-esteem. Yet, with legal segregation finally gone, thanks to the civil rights movement, upwardly mobile black families headed for the suburbs, and many working-class parents believed their children would enjoy a better life than they had.

The vast majority of African Americans who could not afford the luxury of suburban life were left behind in America's overcrowded ghet-

One of the goals of Oscar Williams's Five on the Black Hand Side *was to explore the trials and tribulations of the black middle-class—a subject most black action films, such as* Shaft *and* Superfly, *avoided.*

In 1970, the Black Panthers called for a "Revolutionary People's Constitutional Convention" to rewrite the U.S. Constitution. A photo of Black Panther party chairman Bobby Seale looms over an image of him chained to his chair during his trial on charges of conspiracy to violently disrupt the 1968 Democratic National Convention.

toes. But if leaving was not an option, fighting back certainly was. The first year of the new decade, 1970, was marked by violence, militant campaigns, racial tensions, and new movements demanding social justice. Urban rebellions and police-community violence continued to be a source of tension in several cities, including Philadelphia; New Orleans; New Bedford, Massachusetts; and Hartford, Connecticut. The issue of school desegregation was hardly settled, particularly after court-ordered busing was proposed as a solution to integrate public schools. Throughout the country, white opponents of school integration frequently turned to violence to defend all-white schools. In September 1970, the Black Panther party and activists from the women's and gay liberation movements organized the Revolutionary People's Constitutional Convention, which attracted some 6,000 people to the city of Philadelphia with the goal of rewriting the U.S. Constitution.

THE BLACK PANTHER PARTY CALLS FOR A MASS RALLY AND NATIONAL PRESS CONFERENCE TO ANNOUNCE DATE AND PLACE OF

REVOLUTIONARY PEOPLE'S CONSTITUTIONAL CONVENTION

Lincoln Memorial Washington, D.C. June 19, 1970

For Further Information
Contact NCCF
2327 18th Street N.W,
Washington, D,C, 20009
(202) 265-4418 -4419

The Shackling like a Slave of Black Panther Party Chairman Bobby Seale is like the Reincarnation of Dred Scott 1857. This Brazen Violation of Bobby Seale's Constitutional Rights Exposes Without a Doubt that Black People have No Rights That The Racist Oppressor Is Bound To Respect.

In spite of these events, few black activists and perhaps fewer inner-city residents believed change was inevitable or that the government was on their side. The person African Americans overwhelmingly voted *against* in the 1968 Presidential election, Richard M. Nixon, was now in the White House. A conservative Republican who had lost to John F. Kennedy in the 1960 Presidential race, Nixon attacked welfare mothers, blamed the black poor for their own poverty, and tried to link the social movements of the 1960s to criminals and drug addicts. Nixon's conservative agenda was a far cry from the civil rights movement's vision of a country without poverty or race hatred, a view picked up on and articulated by the man whom Nixon replaced in the White House, Lyndon Baines Johnson.

Yet, Nixon was surprised when he failed to attract black votes during his re-election campaign in 1972. After all, he had appointed a handful of African Americans to mid-level federal posts, and he even called himself a supporter of "black power" when he proposed reducing welfare in favor of grants and tax cuts for black-owned businesses. Despite these measures, very few African Americans trusted Nixon. His cabinet was openly less concerned about racism than the Johnson administration had been. Indeed his domestic advisor, Daniel P. Moynihan, passed on a confidential memo proposing "the time may have come when the issue of race could benefit from a period of 'benign neglect.'" Moynihan felt that enough progress had been made and there was no need to actively combat racial inequities. More important, Nixon and his advisers understood that the Republicans' success came in part because of their attacks on radical social movements, such as the Black Panthers, and on liberal policies, such as Johnson's War on Poverty. A large segment of the white middle class believed that African Americans, especially the poor, received too many government handouts, and they were tired of "paying the bill." Such sentiment was evident to anyone observing George Wallace's Presidential campaign in 1968. A staunch segregationist and former governor of Alabama, Wallace ran as an independent on an extremely conservative and racist platform emphasizing "law and order" and an end to "special privileges" for African Americans. He attracted a huge following among white blue-collar workers, garnering about 13.5 percent of the national vote.

Many white middle- and working-class voters who put Nixon in office supported Wallace in the primary elections. They believed that African Americans had nothing to complain about because, in their view at least, racism no longer existed. They were tired of the Vietnam War and felt besieged by the constant protests by hippies, ghetto residents, feminists, and welfare rights activists. Fearing that ghetto rebellions would spill into their suburbs and that too much of their taxes was going to support welfare, the overwhelming white vote for Nixon partly reflected an anti-black backlash.

One of Nixon's campaign promises was to get rid of "troublemakers," especially militant black nationalist organizations like the Republic of New Afrika, the National Committee to Combat Fascism, the Black Liberation Front, and the Black Panther party—whom Federal Bureau of Investigation (FBI) director J. Edgar Hoover once called "the greatest threat to the internal security of this country." During the Nixon years, the FBI and local police forces intensified their efforts to squelch dissent

Independent Presidential candidate George Wallace, whose extremely conservative platform emphasized "law and order" and ending "special privileges" for African Americans, speaks to his supporters in Fort Worth, Texas, in October 1968. Although "Rage" might be an appropriate characterization of Wallace's campaign, the poster behind him actually says "Courage."

of any kind. And it did not matter if their tactics were legal or not. In Chicago, for example, local police not only raided the headquarters and homes of black activists frequently, they also kept files on prominent outspoken African Americans, including future Presidential candidate the Reverend Jesse Jackson. At the time, Jackson led Operation PUSH (People United to Save Humanity), a fairly mainstream grassroots organization that sought to help African Americans get off welfare, find jobs, and motivate poor children to stay in school.

Jailings, beatings, and constant surveillance conducted by local police and the FBI were part and parcel of what most political movements during this era had to contend with.

One very important case centered around the Reverend Benjamin Chavis, a young black minister of the United Church of Christ who would eventually serve a brief stint as executive director of the National Association for the Advancement of Colored People (NAACP). It all began when Chavis tried to organize a nonviolent campaign in

Wilmington, North Carolina, to improve education for African-American children. The campaign was still in its early stages when, in February 1971, a white-owned store was burned in the midst of the campaign. Chavis, along with eight black student leaders and one white woman activist, was charged and convicted of arson and conspiracy. Altogether, their combined sentences totaled 282 years; the 24-year-old Chavis received 34 of those years. Human rights activists from around the world questioned the convictions from the very beginning. Not only was there no solid evidence against them, but it was revealed that at least one jurist was a member of the Ku Klux Klan—a white supremacist organization with a history of employing violence and intimidation against black people. Even Amnesty International, a worldwide organization dedicated to monitoring human rights abuses, called Benjamin Chavis and his fellow inmates "political prisoners." They quickly became known as the Wilmington Ten.

Benjamin Chavis, one of the Wilmington Ten, spent nearly eight years in prison after being convicted of arson and conspiracy. The conviction was overturned after one of the key witnesses revealed that he had been pressured into lying at the trial.

Despite many appeals, the Wilmington Ten remained in prison throughout most of the decade. Then, in 1977, one of the key witnesses for the state admitted that he had been pressured into lying on the stand. Another witness said he was given a job at a local service station and a minibike in exchange for testimony that would lead to a conviction. Yet, in spite of these new developments in the case, the judge would not reverse the decision. He insisted that the defendants' constitutional rights had not been violated. Yet because of increasingly negative publicity surrounding the case, the governor of North Carolina persuaded prison administrators to parole Chavis in 1979. A year later, the U.S. Court of Appeals overturned the original decision, ruling that the Wilmington Ten had been denied a fair trial.

Many African Americans and movement sympathizers believed that federal, state, and local governments arrested activists on false charges in order to stop them from protesting and organizing. While this may seem to contradict American ideals of freedom, the release of secret files of the FBI's Counter Intelligence Program (COINTELPRO) and the voluminous files local police departments kept on suspected dissidents revealed that some activists were indeed jailed and harassed because of their politics. The FBI devoted much of its energies to collecting infor-

Supporters of the Wilmington Ten take to the streets of Raleigh, North Carolina, to protest their imprisonment. Amnesty International, a worldwide human rights group, considered the group political prisoners.

mation on "radical" organizations. Under COINTELPRO, FBI agents also used fake press releases to spread false rumors about social activists; hired undercover agents to commit crimes in the name of the more militant black power movements; violently attacked competing organizations; and created an atmosphere of tension, confusion, and division within the organizations under surveillance. COINTELPRO was finally disbanded in 1972 after the death of FBI director J. Edgar Hoover. A congressional investigation of the program not only revealed that Hoover had kept tabs on many prominent African Americans—including political leaders Martin Luther King, Jr., Roy Wilkins, and Whitney Young; athletes Muhammad Ali, Joe Louis, Jesse Owens, and Jackie Robinson; and cultural figures such as Lena Horne, Paul Robeson, and James Baldwin—but that President Nixon himself used the FBI to attack his enemies and wage war against alleged dissidents.

Clearly the most celebrated "political prisoner" of the early 1970s was Angela Davis. "Free Angela" posters, buttons, and T-shirts became as much a part of the changing urban landscape as liquor stores and "soul food" restaurants. Tall, lean, with a raised fist and an Afro, a flashing smile, and an aura of confidence—Angela Davis offered the African-

American community a striking image to rally around. To her many supporters—young and old, male and female—she was a young, beautiful, militant intellectual boldly challenging "the system."

Born and raised in Birmingham, Alabama, Angela Davis was the daughter of school teacher and early civil rights activist Sallye Davis. The oldest of three children, Angela Davis lived a fairly comfortable life in some respects, but segregation and racial tensions also made for a very dangerous environment. Two of her friends were killed in a church bombing in September 1963. The bombing was orchestrated by white supremacists retaliating for the civil rights demonstrations in Birmingham. And as a very young child, she lived in a neighborhood where black-owned homes were firebombed so frequently that it was nicknamed "dynamite hill." The bombings were the work of white residents attempting to keep black families out of that section of Birmingham. She remembered one bombing vividly: "I was in the bathroom washing my white shoelaces for Sunday School the next morning when an explosion a hundred times louder than the loudest, most frightening thunderclap I had ever heard shook our house. Medicine bottles fell off the shelves, shattering all around me. The floor seemed to slip away from my feet as I raced in to the kitchen and my frightened mother's arms."

Anxious to leave Birmingham (or "Bombingham" as black residents began calling it), Davis moved to New York City when she was 15 to attend Elisabeth Irwin High School, a renowned experimental private school in Greenwich Village. She went on to Brandeis University, the Sorbonne in Paris, and Goethe University in Frankfurt; in 1967 she moved to California to work toward a Ph.D. in philosophy. Always concerned about the plight of African Americans, she soon became active in the Student Nonviolent Coordinating Committee (SNCC), an organization devoted to challenging racism, fighting for black political power through voter registration, and building links with many of the poorer countries of the world, often called Third World countries because they belonged neither to the rich, industrialized nations of the West (called the First World) nor to the nations of the Communist Bloc (the Second World).

This postcard calling for the release of Angela Davis had the address of the White House printed on the back so that Davis's supporters could write to the President.

As a SNCC activist, Davis saw both the possibilities and limitations of the organization. She not only encountered sexist attitudes on the part of several male leaders, but she realized that SNCC and other black power organizations did not have an adequate explanation for why people remained poor. Insisting that the "free market" (capitalism) exploits workers by paying them poorly and making them dependent on the marketplace and wages to survive, she regarded the capitalist economy as the source of many social ills. Many of her ideas were based on the writings of Karl Marx and Frederick Engels, two 19th-century German radical thinkers whom Davis was introduced to in high school. Reading Marx and Engels' *Communist Manifesto* (1848) as a teenager changed her life. "Like an expert surgeon," she wrote in her autobiography,

> this document cut away cataracts from my eyes. . . . What had seemed a personal hatred of me, an inexplicable refusal of Southern whites to confront their own emotions, and a stubborn willingness of Blacks to acquiesce, became the inevitable consequence of a ruthless system which kept itself alive and well by encouraging spite, competition and the oppression of one group by another. Profit was the word: the cold and constant motive for the behavior, the contempt and the despair I had seen.

Although there are different varieties of Marxism, Marxists generally argue that all wealth is created by labor. Capitalists, or the owners of businesses, are able to exploit labor by denying workers access to other sources of income through the private ownership of land and factories. Thus workers have no choice but to work for wages to survive, a condition which breeds conflict and resentment between those who own wealth and those who do not. Marxists believe that this conflict between workers and owners is a fundamental aspect of capitalist society. To resolve it, they advocate replacing capitalism with "socialism"—a system whereby working people, in theory, share the fruits of their labor. The land and factories would not be owned by private individuals but by the people who work them. The goal of labor would not be to enrich the few, but improve the quality of life for all. Quality education and health care would not be things one would pay for individually but would be paid for and available to all members of society. Of course, there have been attempts to create such a system in places like China and the former Soviet Union, but in these countries it never worked in practice the way it was imagined to work in theory. Nevertheless, in the minds of many Marxists and liberals who sympathized with the Marxist point of view, the failure of socialism in other countries did not diminish the fact that capitalism made some people's lives miserable while making a handful of people very wealthy.

As a Marxist, Davis was convinced that the building of a new social-ist society would go a long way toward creating the kind of equality many labor, student, and civil rights activists dreamed of. Thus in 1969 she made the fateful decision to join the Communist Party of the United States (CPUSA), longtime advocates of socialism whose origins go back to 1919. That same year the University of California at Los Angeles hired her to teach philosophy. However, once her party membership became public knowledge, the California Board of Regents (the body that oversees the University of California campuses) and Governor Ronald Reagan fired her, citing a state law that banned Communists from teaching at state universities.

Davis and the many who rallied to her defense were undoubtedly upset over her dismissal. She challenged the decision in court, arguing

Two years after her release from jail, Angela Davis speaks at the Third World People's Solidarity Conference held at the University of Michigan in 1974.

"Pure nonviolence as a political ideal," wrote George Jackson in his posthumously published book Soledad Brother, *"is absurd: politics is violence. It may serve our purpose to claim nonviolence, but we must never delude ourselves into thinking that we can seize power from a position of weakness, with half measures, polite programs, righteous indignation, or loud entreaties."*

on the basis of the First Amendment that she had the right to freedom of expression. The jury and judge agreed; the law was overturned and the regents were forced to reinstate her. Nevertheless, they eventually succeeded in forcing her out of the University of California system by censuring Davis for her political activism and closely monitoring her classes. Losing her job did not keep her from organizing. She became actively involved with the Black Panther party and worked with radical black prisoners—most notably George Jackson.

George Jackson had been an inmate at Soledad prison in California for nearly a decade when he first came into contact with Davis. After spending the first 14 years of his life in a Chicago ghetto, in 1957 he moved with his family to South Central Los Angeles, where he fell in with neighborhood gangs. He was constantly in trouble with the law; he was arrested several times as a juvenile for theft, burglary, and robbery. At age 15 he was sentenced to eight months at a California Youth Authority camp—a state-run juvenile detention center. He escaped twice from the camp, once fleeing to Illinois, where he was involved in a knifing and subsequently returned to California in chains. Paroled after 16 months, Jackson continued to pursue a life of crime. In February 1961 he was arrested for being an accessory to armed robbery of a gas station in Bakersfield, California. Because no one was hurt and only $70 was taken, the public defender persuaded Jackson to plead guilty in exchange for a light sentence. To his surprise, the judge sentenced him to "one year to life." He was 19 years old.

Jackson was initially sentenced to San Quentin, where he gained a reputation as one of the meanest, toughest inmates in the prison yard. He participated in prison gangs, received disciplinary action at least 47 times for assaulting guards, and was feared by most of his fellow inmates. One of those inmates remembered Jackson as having "had a very bad reputation with the administration as being a black thug, pressuring other prisoners and stuff." But by the fifth or sixth year of his sentence, Jackson began to undergo a dramatic change. Much like Malcolm X, the renowned black nationalist leader who had been assassinated in 1965 and who had spent part of

A black inmate at San Quentin prison receives counseling from a prison official.

his youth in prison, young George Jackson began reading books he had never read in school. And just as Malcolm discovered the Nation of Islam (the Black Muslim movement founded by Elijah Muhammad) in prison, Jackson eventually linked up with the Black Panther party, a militant organization founded in 1966 that advocated armed self-defense, community control of its own police and other city services, and socialism. In his quest to understand why so many of his fellow inmates were black men, why so many were driven to steal, he studied the writings of revolutionary leaders from across the globe and read broadly in the fields of history, sociology, and politics. He came to the conclusion that racism, the economy, and the government's covert efforts to put a lid on black rebellion were the main reasons for the rise in African-American prisoners. In one sense, he argued, virtually all of the inmates were "political prisoners":

> There are still some blacks here who consider themselves criminals—but not many. Believe me, my friend, with the time and incentive that these brothers have to read, study, and think, you will find no class or category more aware, more embittered, desperate, or dedicated to the ultimate remedy—revolution. . . . They live like there was no tomorrow.

By the late 1960s, Jackson emerged as one of Soledad's most outspoken radicals. He introduced fellow prisoners to a variety of radical ideas, including Marxism and black nationalism—the idea that black people made up a nation within the U.S. and should work to create and control their own institutions. Influenced by the various protest movements erupting outside prison walls, Jackson and a few of his fellow convicts set out to "transform the black criminal mentality into a black revolutionary mentality." Quickly, prison authorities identified him as a serious threat when he attempted to organize the inmates to fight for better conditions.

In 1969, the activities and plight of George Jackson became nationally known after he and two fellow inmates, Fleeta Drumgo and John Clutchette, were accused of murdering a prison guard. Since the state had very little evidence against the three men, most of their supporters believed they were being framed for political reasons. Jackson, Drumgo, and Clutchette were well known in Soledad for their political activism. Once the case went public, they became known as the Soledad Brothers. Throughout the country, student activists, black militants, and people concerned about prisoners' rights organized demonstrations demanding the release of the Soledad Brothers. Donations for their legal defense came from all over the country. Leading publications, including the *New York Times Magazine,* carried articles about Jackson and the others. Within a few months, they were celebrities. Their most vocal defenders included actress Jane Fonda, child psychiatrist Benjamin Spock, and poet Allen Ginsberg.

The Soledad Brothers' most dedicated advocate turned out to be George Jackson's younger brother Jonathan, also a close acquaintance of Angela Davis's. On August 7, 1970, the younger Jackson, barely 17 years old, somehow smuggled several guns into the Marin County (California)

Courthouse during the trial of James McClain, another black Soledad prisoner accused of stabbing a guard. After watching the proceedings from the audience for a while, Jonathan Jackson rose to his feet, drew a sawed-off shotgun from under his coat and announced, "All right, gentlemen. I'm taking over now." He then passed the other guns he had concealed to McClain and Ruchell Magee, a Soledad inmate who had been brought to trial as a witness to the stabbing. They took the judge, the deputy district attorney, and three jurors hostage in a van parked

George Jackson's funeral on August 28, 1971, attracted more than 1,000 people, many of whom gave the black power salute as Jackson's body was taken from the church.

outside. As they left the courthouse, according to one witness, McClain shouted, "Free or Release the Soledad Brothers by 12:30 or they all die!" The police and San Quentin guards in the area responded promptly. Remaining true to their "no hostage" policy, the guards opened fire on the van as it pulled off. When the smoke cleared Jonathan, along with two prisoners and the judge, lay dead. (Soon after the Soledad Brothers were acquitted of murder, prison guards killed George Jackson during an alleged escape attempt. The guards claimed Jackson had hidden a gun in his Afro.)

Young Jonathan Jackson's actions directly affected Angela Davis. The guns he used were hers—firearms he had taken without permission. Because Davis owned the guns and because she was a noted radical activist in California, the FBI issued a warrant for her arrest and placed her on its "Ten Most Wanted" list. Following her capture, an international campaign demanding her release was born. Even the celebrated soul singer Aretha Franklin offered to pay her bail: "I'm going to set Angela free . . . not because I believe in communism but because she's a Black woman who wants freedom for all Black people." After spending 18 months in jail, she was finally released in February 1972 on $102,000 bail. She was eventually acquitted of all charges.

The decade of the 1970s, therefore, was hardly the end of a militant era. The violent repression and jailings of black radicals no doubt transformed the movements they led, sometimes making leaders ineffective, other times turning them into martyrs. New debates and new circumstances compelled African-American activists to think about politics in new ways. African-American women activists began to chart their own course, creating a dynamic black feminist movement that challenged male-dominated black nationalism and white-dominated women's rights organizations. Moreover, black elected officials joined community activists and artists to develop a new approach to the ballot.

CHAPTER 2
"IT'S NATION TIME!"
FROM BLACK FEMINISM TO BLACK CAUCUS

◇ ◇ ◇

The Reverend Jesse Jackson (left) and Richard Hatcher, mayor of Gary, Indiana, acknowledge the crowd during the opening ceremony for the National Black Political Assembly in 1972.

Black community activist Margaret Wright was tired of being told by male leaders in the black power movement that black women oppressed black men, that black women were domineering, that successful black women stripped black men of their manhood. "Black women aren't oppressing them," she announced in a 1970 interview. "We're helping them get their liberation. It's the white man who's oppressing, not us. All we ever did was scrub floors so they could get their little selves together!" The very idea that black women kept black men down made her even more angry when she thought about the role most black women had to play in the civil rights and black liberation movements. "We run errands, lick stamps, mail letters, and do the door-to-door. But when it comes to the speaker's platform, it's all men up there blowing their souls, you dig."

Margaret Wright knew the truth. Black women, in general, were not only more exploited and oppressed than black men but they were often oppressed *by* black men. As an activist in the Los Angeles–based group Women Against Repression, she confronted issues ranging from wife battering to inequities in household chores. Most black women not only worked for wages but were responsible for child care, cooking, and cleaning. And when it came to participating in political movements, black women were often shunted aside or told that the struggle for liberation is "a man's job." While she acknowledged that black men and white women were also oppressed, she wanted both groups to understand how they unintentionally contributed to the exploitation of black women:

> Black women have been doubly oppressed. On the job, we're low women on the totem pole. White women have their problems. They're interviewed for secretarial instead of the executive thing. But we're interviewed for mopping floors and stuff like that. Sometimes we have to take what's left over in Miss Ann's refrigerator. This is all exploitation. And when we get home from work, the old man is wondering why his greens aren't cooked on time.

Margaret Wright voiced the opinions of a growing number of African-American women, some of whom joined forces with the feminist movement that had reemerged in the 1960s. While there was no single definition of feminism, most feminists agreed that male domination—in the family and the government—pushed women into an inferior status in society. They argued that women were paid less for the same job, underrepresented in positions of power and authority, and expected to take responsibility for housework and other domestic duties, not because they were less able than men, but because they were discriminated against.

Even the culture women lived in contributed to their subordination. Women were portrayed as passive and weak or as sex objects for male pleasure. Feminists did not merely want to take men's places in positions of power, to substitute male dominance with female dominance; they fought to replace male domination with a more just, equitable society. As Margaret Wright put it, "Men are chauvinistic. I don't want to be chauvinistic. Some women run over people in the business world, doing the same thing as men. I don't want to compete on no damned exploitative level. I don't want to exploit nobody."

Of course, Wright and her compatriots were not the first generation of black feminists. Black women had been fighting for freedom, equality, and power since their arrival on these shores. Black women actively contributed to the women's rights movements of the 19th and early 20th centuries—even if white feminists did not embrace black women as their sisters. But the fight against sexism and the growing impoverishment of African-American women took on new vigor in the early 1970s.

Ironically, this new wave of black feminism was partly a response to male chauvinism within the civil rights, black power, and student movements of the period. Many cultural nationalists—activists who believed that black people in the United States should adopt traditional

Black women struggled against the sexism they encountered within the civil rights, black power, and student movements. Black working-class women were also ignored by mainstream feminist organizations, which focused on removing barriers to women in white-collar professions.

African cultures—emphasized that women ought to remain in "their place." One pamphlet distributed by a nationalist organization in Newark laid out, in no uncertain terms, what men and women's roles should be: "It is only reasonable that the man be the head of the house because he is able to defend and protect the development of his home. . . . Women cannot do the same things as men—they are made by nature to function differently. Equality of men and women is something that cannot happen even in the abstract world." Of course, not all male advocates of black nationalism were hopelessly sexist; on the contrary, some opposed statements such as these. Moreover, not all black women active in nationalist movements agreed with this sort of logic. Women frequently challenged such remarks. Nevertheless, the overall tenor of the black power movement emphasized the struggle for power, equality, and rights as a struggle for "manhood."

Concerned about the rising tide of black male sexism and chauvinism, many African-American women active in political and social movements spoke out. Toni Cade Bambara, a writer and activist who edited an important anthology in 1970 titled *The Black Woman,* wrote: "We rap about being correct but ignore the danger of having one of our population regard the other with such condescension and perhaps fear that that half finds it necessary to 'reclaim his manhood' by denying her her peoplehood." Some African-American women were drawn to mainstream feminist organizations, such as the National Organization for Women (NOW), or small radical feminist groups such as the Redstockings and WITCH. However, during the early to mid-1970s, most black feminists avoided the predominantly white women's movement. Several leading white feminists, including Susan Brownmiller, Jo Freeman, and Kathie Sarachild, had cut their political teeth in the civil rights struggles of the early to mid-1960s and compared the oppression of women with the oppression of African Americans. But many black feminists found their white counterparts unaware of the importance of race and racism, and some resented the way white women equated their plight with black people. When white women appealed to sisterhood, African-American women were quick to point out that historically their relations with one another had been as domestic servants (or other employees) to employers. More importantly, most black women activists did not separate their fight for women's rights from issues affecting the entire black community. The majority of black feminists did not believe, as many of their white counterparts did, that all men were the enemy.

A participant at a NOW regional conference in Atlantic City in 1974. Most black women remained suspicious of mainstream organizations such as NOW, which they thought ignored the effects of racism on black women.

In 1973 several African-American women's groups were founded, the most important of which was the National Black Feminist Organization (NBFO). The first NBFO conference was held in New York City and was attended by approximately 400 African-American women. The atmosphere was electric; no one attending the conference had ever witnessed such a large gathering of black women speaking about issues that directly affected them. It became clear from the speeches that the NBFO's emphasis would be on combating sexist and racist discrimination against black women and struggling for greater involvement in the political process. Many journalists and activists took special note of the diversity of participants—black women from all walks of life, from domestic workers to lawyers, welfare rights organizers to polished elected officials. Although the different backgrounds of these women enriched the discussion from the floor, it also created tensions. After its first year, black women active in the welfare rights movements began to feel that the NBFO sidestepped the problems of poor women, and many African-American lesbians criticized the NBFO for ignoring

Members of the National Black Feminist Organization gather at a NOW meeting in 1973. Some members of the NBFO believed that their organization did not represent the interests of working-class women or lesbians, and formed a radical organization known as the Combahee River Collective.

homophobia (fear of, and discrimination against, homosexuals) and for speaking only to issues affecting heterosexual women. Partly in response to the NBFO's shortcomings, new black women's groups were formed to address issues that the NBFO did not choose to address, such as homophobia and the replacement of capitalism with socialism.

Despite such differences, black politics in the 1970s—as in the 1960s—emphasized unity above all else. With unity came strength, black political leaders argued, and with strength came real power. Nowhere was the potential for real power more evident than in electoral politics. After the Voting Rights Act of 1965 was passed, and organizations like SNCC waged massive voter registration campaigns, the ballot seemed to be an increasingly powerful weapon. Changes in the racial makeup of cities, in particular, improved chances for African Americans to gain a stronger political foothold in major urban centers.

In some cases, these political challenges proved successful. The mayoral victories of Carl Stokes in Cleveland and Richard Hatcher in Gary, Indiana, in 1967 raised black hopes that electoral politics might offer real opportunities, at least at the municipal level. However, despite a growing number of black voters in the nation's cities, African Americans held few really important political offices. During the early 1970s, for example, black elected officials tended to hold low-level municipal and county posts, especially in the areas of law enforcement, school boards, and some city councils. Most of these black elected officials were in the South. The lack of black political representation in big cities, where African Americans made up 40 to 50 percent of the population, was particularly striking. To overcome this imbalance, black political leaders worked hard to devise strategies to win local elections.

The need for a fresh, dynamic political strategy led to the formation of the Congressional Black Caucus (CBC) in 1971, a group of black members of Congress committed to working jointly in the interests of African Americans. The origins of the CBC go back to 1969, when Congressman Charles Diggs of Detroit led a committee of nine black representatives to oppose President Nixon's policies. The CBC initially worked for reforms in job training, health care, welfare and social services, and other areas of social policy that directly affected African-American communities. It also tried to fashion a national strategy to increase black political representation. The formation of the CBC attracted a wide range of political activists, including cultural nationalists such as Imamu Amiri Baraka, the popular playwright and poet whose Newark, New Jersey-based movement, New Ark, had just played a key role in electing that city's first black mayor in 1970. Like many other progressives, Baraka believed that the CBC and black voters could pressure the Democratic party into becoming more accountable to black people. For Baraka and other radical supporters of the CBC, however, the ultimate goal was not to have more influence over the Democratic party. Rather, they wanted to build an independent black political movement.

The idea of a national black political campaign generated a lot of excitement among black artists as well as among elected officials and community activists. Although black writers, musicians, and visual artists

Richard Hatcher (top) of Gary, Indiana, and Carl Stokes of Cleveland, Ohio, were among the first blacks to be elected mayors of major U.S. cities.

The Congressional Black Caucus was formed in 1971 by a group of black members of Congress committed to working for the interests of black Americans. Members of the caucus attending this press conference included Shirley Chisholm (far left) and Charles Rangel (far right).

had a long tradition of linking politics and art, the generation of black artists that emerged in the '60s and '70s set a new standard for their direct political involvement and community activism. Poets such as Baraka, Don L. Lee (Haki Madhubuti), Mari Evans, Kalamu ya Salaam, and Sonia Sanchez were among the leading voices calling for a coordinated black political movement. Thus, prompted by Baraka and Richard Hatcher, mayor of Gary, Indiana, several African-American political leaders organized a national convention to create a black agenda and to discuss possible strategies for gaining greater black political power. The idea proved enormously popular, and throughout the fall and winter of 1971, grassroots political movements elected delegates, people raised money for transportation, and political activists passed out leaflets informing local communities about the event.

In March 1972, some 8,000 African Americans (3,000 of whom were official delegates) arrived in Gary, Indiana, to attend the first convention of the National Black Political Assembly, which was more commonly known as the "Gary Convention." The roll call, the tall floor signs identifying each state's delegates, the constant calls to order were much like the Democratic or Republican conventions we see on television. But the comparison stopped there; at Gary all the faces were black and many were working class. And this sea of 8,000 black faces was chanting, "It's Nation Time! It's Nation Time!" No one in that room had ever seen anything like this before.

The feeling among the delegates that it was, indeed, "Nation Time" captures the political sensibilities dominating the convention. The radical black nationalists clearly won the day; moderates who supported integration and backed the Democratic party were in the minority. Most of the delegates—at least the most vocal ones—agreed that African-American communities faced a social and economic crisis, and that nothing short of fundamental changes in the political and economic system could bring an end to this crisis. As the famous Gary Declaration put it:

> A Black political convention, indeed all truly Black politics, must begin from this truth: *The American system does not work for the masses of our people, and it cannot be made to work without radical, fundamental changes.* (Indeed, this system does not really work in favor of the humanity of anyone in America.) . . .
>
> The challenge is thrown to us here in Gary. *It is the challenge to consolidate and organize our own Black role as the vanguard in the struggle for a new society.* To accept that challenge is to move to independent Black politics. There can be no equivocation on that issue. History leaves us no other choice. White politics has not and cannot bring the changes we need.

The convention's agenda included a bill that would expand voter registration and provisions to ensure community control over such institutions as police, government, and city services.

To arrive at such a radical document was not easy. From the very outset local issues clashed with efforts to create a national agenda, and delegates representing different outlooks had trouble compromising. Indeed, part of the Michigan delegation walked out of the convention to protest the separatist tone of the resolutions. Most elected officials also believed the delegates had gone too far: resolutions were passed calling for the creation of independent black schools and opposing court-ordered busing. And, as politicians active in the Democratic party, they strongly rejected the pledge to create an independent black political party.

Gary was an amazing example of democracy at work. Most mainstream political leaders and elected officials did not expect such a radical agenda to come out of this convention. But the 3,000 official delegates and the additional 5,000 in the audience believed they had a voice, a right to express their thoughts on black liberation.

The National Black Political Assembly drew more than 5,000 delegates, from all 50 states, to Gary, Indiana in 1972.

Unfortunately, the vision created in Gary was soon abandoned. First, grassroots activists committed to the Gary Declaration did not have national visibility. Black elected officials and leaders who did have that visibility were concerned with being reelected or losing white allies. Therefore, most black elected officials did not dare echo Gary's call for revolutionary changes in American society. Besides, many black politicians felt betrayed by the convention. They dismissed the delegates for being insensitive to and ignorant of the kind of "hard-nosed" negotiations black elected officials must participate in. Real politics, they argued, involved compromising and coalition building, not demands for revolutionary change.

By the time the 1972 Presidential election campaign was well underway, the historic Gary Convention seemed to be but a faint echo in the world of electoral politics. Most black politicians scrambled to endorse white Democrats, either Hubert Humphrey or George McGovern, for the Presidential nomination. Others, like Floyd McKissick, a black power proponent and head of the Congress of Racial Equality (CORE), joined fellow CORE leaders and endorsed Republican Richard Nixon. In particular, Nixon's support for black business and his advocacy of self-help appealed to CORE leaders, whose politics had grown increasingly conservative. Meanwhile, amid the backroom negotiating and political deals being made between white men and black men, an African-American congresswoman from New York stepped to the fore and sought the Democratic party's nomination for President.

Shirley Chisholm's bid for President surprised everyone. She certainly did not develop a reputation as a radical outside the political process. Indeed, she joined those who abandoned the original goals of the National Black Political Assembly, and in fact felt betrayed by parts of the Gary Declaration. And yet, she was not your typical politician. Born Shirley St. Hill in Brooklyn in 1924 and raised by working-class Barbadian parents, Chisholm earned a bachelor's degree from Brooklyn College and an M.A. in early childhood education from Columbia University. After several frustrating years as an active member of the Democratic party in the Bedford-Stuyvesant section of Brooklyn, in 1968 she ran against former CORE leader James Farmer (who by then had joined the Republican party) for a newly created congressional seat representing Brooklyn. She soundly beat Farmer, becoming the first black woman elected to the House of Representatives. Her active support for

Congresswoman Shirley Chisholm speaks at a pro-choice rally in New York City in 1972. In 1968 Chisholm became the first black woman elected to the House of Representatives.

equal rights, affirmative action policies, and women's liberation attracted the attention of both women's organizations and civil rights advocates. She turned out to be among the most outspoken feminists in Congress, serving as an active member of the National Organization for Women, a founder of the National Women's Political Caucus, and member of the National Abortion Rights Action League. In a memorable speech delivered at the Conference on Women's Employment organized by the Congressional Committee on Education and Labor, Chisholm called on women to "rebel."

> Women in this country must become revolutionaries. We must refuse to accept the old, the traditional roles and stereotypes. . . . We must replace the old, negative thoughts about our femininity with positive thoughts and positive action affirming it, and more. But we must also remember that we will be breaking with tradition, and so we must prepare ourselves educationally, economically, and psychologically in order that we will be able to accept and bear with the sanctions that society will immediately impose upon us.

Shirley Chisholm thanks her supporters after her failed bid for the Presidency during the 1972 Democratic National Convention in Miami.

Thus, when Chisholm made her bid for the Presidency in 1972, she was poised, experienced, and knowledgeable about issues affecting African Americans and women. And she earned supporters. On the first ballot she garnered over 150 votes at the Democratic National Convention. But, to her surprise and disappointment, very few white women's organizations, black male politicians, or black organizations led by men came out in support of her candidacy. Chisholm was disillusioned by black male politicians who refused to take her campaign seriously precisely because she was a woman. The only major black political organization to endorse her candidacy was the Black Panther party, which by then had a substantial number of women in leadership positions.

Chisholm lost the nomination to George McGovern, who was then summarily crushed in the 1972 election. Nixon's popularity had soared, especially among white working- and middle-class voters. After all, he promised to be tough on crime and extra hard on dissidents. Ironically, Nixon's own administration harbored a number of crooks, and the President himself seemed to be the ringleader. Less than a year after his reelection a Senate investigation revealed that Nixon directed or had knowledge about a whole litany of crimes against political rivals, including the June 1972 break-in at the campaign headquarters of the Democratic National Committee. On August 9, 1974, just before the House of Representatives was to vote on impeachment, Nixon resigned. The Watergate affair ended in the first resignation of a President in U.S. history, the imprisonment of 25 Nixon aides, and a crisis in American politics.

Watergate was a serious blow to the rising hopes that many African Americans had placed in electoral politics. For others it confirmed what they already believed: the white-dominated political system was corrupt and completely bankrupt. A few activists tried to resurrect the political spirit of the Gary Convention by continuing to support a path independent of the Democrats and Republicans. But the very idea of an independent black political party, which had inspired the Gary Convention in the first place, was no longer a goal. Indeed, it would be another four years before a national black independent political party was formed. The National Black Political Assembly drew only 1,000 delegates to its third national convention in 1976. One year later, its membership had shrunk to a paltry 300. Political apathy and cynicism was also evident in the declining number of African Americans willing to vote. The percentage of voting age blacks who actually went to the polls dropped from 52.1 percent in 1972 to 49 percent in 1976.

By the time the United States geared up for its bicentennial celebration in 1976, African Americans had reason to look upon the democratic process with mixed feelings. They had certainly made progress in the electoral sphere. In 1969, 994 black men and 131 black women held public office nationwide; by 1975 the number of black elected officials grew to 2,973 men and 530 women. Black politicians won mayoral races in several major cities, including Los Angeles, Atlanta, New Orleans, Philadelphia, and Washington, D.C. By 1974, more than 200 African Americans served as state legislators, and 17 sat in Congress—including four women, Shirley Chisholm, Cardiss Collins of Illinois, Barbara Jordan of Texas, and Yvonne Brathwaite Burke of California. For all the pessimism surrounding Presidential races, municipal victories were greeted with optimism.

These were victories for black politics, for sure, but bittersweet ones. Once the victory parties were over, many residents still had a diffi-

MS. CHIS.
FOR
PRES.

A campaign button from Shirley Chisholm's attempt to secure the Presidential nomination. Although she lost, Chisholm made history by becoming the first African American to seek the Democratic nomination for President. Unfortunately, very few established black male politicians supported her campaign.

Congresswoman Barbara Jordan, who represented the 18th Congressional District of Houston, Texas, in the House of Representatives from 1972 to 1978, at the 1976 Democratic National Convention, where she delivered the keynote address.

cult time obtaining city services, affordable housing, or improved schools. In some cases, local politicians consciously tied their fate to big business. Some black citizens began to question whether having an African American in city hall even made a difference. But most black mayors really wanted to help the communities that put them into office. What they had not counted on was a reduction in federal spending on cities, white and black middle-class flight to the suburbs, a rapid growth in urban poverty and unemployment, and one of the most severe economic recessions in U.S. history.

CHAPTER 3

Inner City Blues
Urban Poverty in the 1970s

◇ ◇ ◇

North Lawndale was once a thriving Chicago community made up of European immigrants and U.S.-born whites and blacks. A community of working-class neighborhoods, North Lawndale before 1970 was home to people who worked for International Harvester, Western Electric, Sears Roebuck, Zenith, Sunbeam, or any one of several other factories and retail outlets in the area. By 1980, most of these firms had closed up shop, leaving empty lots and burned-out buildings in their wake. One resident nostalgically remembered North Lawndale's thriving local business community: "We had an auto center and banks, a York's department store, a Woolworth's. Roosevelt and Kedzie were both such good shopping streets. We had all kinds of specialty shops. There were grocery stores all up and down the street, an A & P and that Dell Farm food market." But those days were over. The dominant retail outlets by the early 1980s were bars and liquor stores. In less than a generation, North Lawndale's economy had evaporated, leaving 58 percent of its able-bodied workers unemployed and half of its population on welfare. As jobs disappeared, so did most of the white and black middle-class residents. Once a thriving industrial hub, North Lawndale became one of the poorest black ghettos in Chicago.

The story of North Lawndale was repeated in almost every major city in the United States after 1970. What are the reasons for such economic devastation? Why has the collapse of the urban economy had such

Burned-out buildings like this one in Philadelphia symbolized the poverty that swept across the inner cities of the United States during the 1970s.

a profound impact on African Americans? To answer these questions, we need to first acknowledge that the economies under the free enterprise system have always had their ups and downs. Sometimes manufacturers produce more than the market can absorb, which not only results in lower prices but leads many companies to fire excess workers. Other times new technology intended to make production faster and more efficient leads to layoffs or reduced wages because new machinery often requires workers with less skill. These and other worldwide economic conditions have caused the U.S. economy to swing between economic surges and periods of economic recessions or outright depressions. And in virtually every case of recession, as we have seen in previous volumes, African-American workers were the "last hired and first fired."

But by the mid-1970s, parts of the U.S. economy appeared to be in a permanent crisis. Ironically, just as programs were being implemented to correct racial imbalances in the workplace, and laws barring discrimination in hiring were being enforced a little more vigorously than before, much of the manufacturing part of the economy began a downward cycle from which it never seemed to recover. Even if protection for black workers improved slightly, changes in the global economy created massive unemployment and led to an expansion of poverty among African Americans not seen since the Great Depression of the 1930s.

A series of events and policies during the early 1970s contributed to the decline of the U.S. economy, especially its heavy industry—steelmaking and the manufacture of automobiles, tires, textiles, and machines of various kinds. In 1973, the Organization of Petroleum Exporting Countries (OPEC), an alliance of mostly Arab oil-producing countries that joined together in 1960 to reduce competition and set higher oil prices,

As factories and stores left the inner cities during the 1970s, the one business that managed to thrive was the liquor store.

The line at a New York City welfare office in 1971. With one out of every three black families living below the poverty line, it should not be surprising that the welfare rolls swelled during the 1970s.

declared an embargo on oil shipments to the United States and Western Europe to protest Israel's war with its Arab neighbors. Because the United States had become dependent on foreign oil supplies, the embargo had a devastating impact on the economy, making it difficult for individual consumers and big business to obtain inexpensive fuels. Plants shut down in large numbers. In 1974 alone, sales and manufacturing of American automobiles declined drastically, unemployment nearly doubled, and inflation more than doubled. Over the next 10 years the economy never really recovered; the value of imported manufactured goods from places like Japan and Western Europe grew from less than 14 percent of the U.S. domestic economy in 1970 to almost 40 percent in 1979, while at the same time inflation, which is an indication of the amount of money needed to buy goods, sharply increased. With increased inflation came a steady loss in the standard of living for all Americans.

President Nixon tried to control inflation, but his policies actually made matters worse, especially for the poor. First, in August 1971 he temporarily froze wages, prices, and rents. But because prices and rents were already high, those earning low wages found themselves in the same situation as before. Second, Nixon placed a tariff—an additional import tax—on Japanese-made cars. This was intended to reduce competition between Japanese auto manufacturers and American manufacturers, but all it did was increase the price of otherwise affordable Japanese economy cars. American-made cars, for the most part, were still rather expensive and tended to use more gas than foreign cars. And in an economy in which oil prices were rising faster than just about any other item, cars that required less gas continued to be popular in the United States.

In spite of Nixon's measures, inflation continued to rise rapidly and low wages and growing unemployment made it impossible for large numbers of consumers to buy American products, no matter how much government tried to protect the market with tariffs. Moreover, massive military spending exacerbated the country's economic woes. It dramatically increased the national debt and redirected much-needed investment away from roads, schools, and industries unrelated to the military buildup. Just months before President Nixon signed a peace agreement withdrawing U.S. troops from Vietnam, the national deficit had grown to $40 billion.

President Richard Nixon gathered all of the black appointees to his administration for a meeting at the White House on March 5, 1970.

President Gerald Ford continued Nixon's economic policies, and when Democrat Jimmy Carter took over the Presidency in 1976, the situation for African Americans improved only slightly. He appointed Patricia Harris, an African-American woman, as Secretary of Housing and Urban Development, and Andrew Young, a black veteran of the civil rights movement, as ambassador to the United Nations. The Carter administration did little to lessen unemployment, and the jobless rate for African Americans increased during his first two years in office. Like the Republican presidents before him, Carter gave corporations a big tax cut, reduced financial aid to black colleges and universities, provided minuscule support for the nation's declining cities, and slashed federal spending for social programs—notably welfare, free lunch programs for children, and health services. He even backpedaled on his promise to reduce defense spending: the military budget for 1978 reached $111.8 billion, the highest level in U.S. history up to that point.

The creation of multinational corporations in the post–World War II era was the most important change in the new global economy. These multinational corporations no longer had a stake in staying in a particular country or region. Instead, they moved their firms wherever labor and taxes were cheaper, pollution laws were less stringent, and labor unions were either weak or nonexistent. Some manufacturers moved from the Midwest and Northeast to the southern United States in search of cheaper labor with weaker unions, although the South hardly experienced an economic boom during the 1970s. The more common trend was for big companies to set up shop in countries like Mexico, Brazil, and South Africa, leaving in their wake empty American factories and huge numbers of unemployed workers. By 1979, for example, 94 percent of the profits of the Ford Motor Company and 63 percent of the profits from Coca-Cola came from overseas operations. Between 1973 and 1980, at least 4 million U.S. jobs were lost when firms moved their operations to foreign countries. And during the decade of the 1970s, at least 32 million jobs were lost as a result of shutdowns, relocations, and scaling-back operations.

The decline of manufacturing jobs in steel, rubber, auto, and other heavy industries had a devastating impact on black workers. Although black joblessness had been about twice that of whites since the end of World War II, black unemployment rates increased even more rapidly, especially after 1971. During these economic downturns, white unemployment tended to be temporary, with a higher percentage of white workers returning to work. For blacks, layoffs were often permanent. Mary Morgan, a steel worker who had been laid off after 10 years of service, could not find work after 18 months of constant searching. "I haven't been able to find anything else," she told an interviewer in 1983. "And all my benefits is ran out, even my little savings. My children help a little. I have six—all grown now. They're all unemployed. Three of them worked at one company that was sort of like the mill. It's all but closed down now. They had been going on unemployment and trying to find a job, but that has ran out now." Mary Morgan's story is reflected in the statistics: while the number of unemployed white workers declined by 562,000 between 1975 and 1980, the number of black unemployed *increased* by 200,000 during this period—the widest unemployment gap between blacks and whites since the government started keeping such statistics.

The loss of well-paying industrial jobs affected not only African Americans but the entire working class. Some workers looked to labor unions affiliated with the American Federation of Labor–Congress of

A city employee on strike outside a San Francisco cable car barn in 1970. During the 1970s, many blacks looked to labor unions to protect their rights and advance their interests.

Industrial Organizations (AFL-CIO) to battle factory closures and wage reductions. Labor unions were created to protect workers and advance their interests. By organizing collectively in unions, workers can force employers to improve their wages, benefits, hours, and working environment by threatening to strike. But labor unions are effective only when the majority of workers in a particular industry or firm join.

At the height of the recession in the 1970s, however, most labor unions were on the defensive, fighting desperately to hold on to the gains they had made a decade earlier. To make matters worse, many black industrial workers felt that white labor leaders were not very responsive to their needs. These leaders did not actively promote African Americans to leadership positions within the unions. In 1982, for example, the AFL-CIO's 35-member Executive Council had only two black members, a figure that fell far short of representing actual black membership. Indeed, African Americans tended to have higher rates of participation than whites in union activities: by 1983, more than 27 percent of black workers were union members compared to about 19 percent of white workers.

Politically, the AFL-CIO leadership took stands that openly went against the interests of the majority of black workers. In 1972 George Meany supported Nixon's bid for the Presidency, which was interpreted by black rank-and-file members as a clear sign that the AFL-CIO was deserting African Americans. In response, a group of black trade union activists formed the Coalition of Black Trade Unionists (CBTU) in 1972. Under the leadership of veteran labor organizer William Lucy, secretary-treasurer of the American Federation of State, County, and Municipal Employees (AFSCME), the CBTU not only condemned the Nixon administration for what it felt were racist policies, but attacked AFL-CIO president George Meany for endorsing Nixon. The CBTU also issued a statement critical of union leaders who did not actively oppose discrimination and support minority and rank-and-file efforts to have a greater voice in the affairs of the union.

The loss of manufacturing positions was accompanied by an expansion of low-wage service jobs. The more common service jobs included retail clerks, janitors, maids, data processors, security guards, waitresses, and cooks—jobs with little or no union representation. Not everyone who was laid off in the 1970s and 1980s got these kinds of jobs, and those who did experienced substantial reductions in their income. Many of

In 1972, William Lucy, a veteran labor organizer, helped to form the Coalition of Black Trade Unionists (CBTU). Here, Lucy addresses the 1973 CBTU convention.

these new service jobs paid much less than manufacturing jobs. They tended to be part-time and offered very little in the way of health or retirement benefits.

Black men and women who were laid off from auto plants and steel mills in the Midwest and South suddenly found themselves working at fast food and sanitation jobs to make ends meet. Young people entering the job market for the first time quickly discovered that the opportunities their parents once had were fading quickly. Many African-American youths without the option to go to college chose the military as an alternative to low-wage service work. As the United States pulled out of Vietnam, the military became one of the biggest employers of African Americans: the percentage of blacks in the armed forces rose from 18 percent in 1972 to 33 percent in 1979.

These dramatic changes in the economy meant greater poverty for African Americans. One of the most striking features of the 1970s was the widening income gap between blacks and whites. At the beginning of the decade, African Americans in the northeastern United States made about 71 cents for every dollar whites made; by 1979 that ratio dropped to 58 cents. In 1978, 30.6 percent of black families earned income below the official poverty line, compared with 8.7 percent of white families.

Black women and children were the hardest hit by the economic crisis. Hemmed in by limited job opportunities, more and more working-class black women found themselves having to raise children without the benefit of a spouse to help pay the bills or participate in child care. The number of black homes without male wage earners rose from 22 percent in 1960 to 35 percent in 1975. Since black women, especially those in their teens and 20s, were the lowest paid and had the highest unemployment rate, it is not an accident that black single-mother households headed the list of families below the poverty line. In 1969, 54 percent of all black families below the poverty line were headed by women; in 1974 this figure rose to 67 percent.

Several politicians and academics blame the rising number of "female-headed households" for the decline of inner cities and the rise of black crime and violence. This crisis of the black family, they argue, is new and unprecedented. They insist that the inability of single mothers to control and discipline their children, combined with the lack of male role models, has led to a whole generation of out-of-control youth. But a lot of these claims are based on misinformation. First of all, single-mother families are not a uniquely "black" crisis; between 1970 and 1987 the birth rate for white unwed mothers rose by 77 percent. Second, out-of-wedlock births are not entirely new to African-American communities. Studies have shown that at least since the days of slavery black women are more likely than white women to bear children outside of marriage and to marry at later ages, after becoming mothers. Part of the reason has to do with the fact that black families have tended not to ostracize women for out-of-wedlock births.

Why have the number of female-headed households grown, and what impact has it had on the social and economic fabric of black communities? First, the declining number of employed black men has contributed to the growth of single-parent households. Aside from a rapid increase in permanently unemployed black men who suddenly cannot support their families as they had in the past, black men have a higher chance of dying young than any other male population in the United States. They are more often victims of occupational accidents, fatal diseases, and homicides than other men. And throughout the 1970s and 1980s, the black male prison population increased threefold; by 1989, 23 percent of black males ages 20 to 29, or almost one out of every four, were either behind bars or on legal probation or parole. Another important factor is that African Americans have a higher divorce and separation rate than whites. High unemployment for black males certainly contributes to marital instability among poor families, but welfare policies also play a major role. In at least 25 states, two-parent families are ineligible for Aid to Families with Dependent Children (AFDC), and in many cases black men have to leave the household in order for the women and children to have access to welfare and Medicaid—a state-funded program to provide free health care to the needy.

Mae Boston (right) used part of her welfare check to cover the cost of day-care for her daughter Laurie so that she could take part in a job-training program.

Although single-parent families (including those run by males) tended to suffer more than two-parent families because they lacked a second wage earner, the structure of the family was not the *cause* of poverty. Most of these households were poor not because the women were unmarried but because of the lack of employment opportunities for women, lower levels of education, and the gross inequality in wages as a result of race and sex discrimination. One study shows, for example, that while 75 percent of unemployed black women heading families were poor in 1977, only 27 percent of employed black women heading families were poor. Besides, the vast majority of women who ended up as single parents were poor *before* they had children or experienced divorce, separation, or the death of their husband.

Finally, single-parent families are not always the product of economic deprivation. Oftentimes they reflect the efforts of black women to escape abusive situations and to raise their children in a more supportive environment. As Barbara Omolade, an African-American scholar and activist, explained it: "My children and other children of Black single mothers are better people because they do not have to live in families where violence, sexual abuse, and emotional estrangement are the daily, hidden reality. . . . In a society where men are taught to dominate and women to follow, we all have a lot to overcome in learning to build relationships, with each other and with our children, based on love and justice. For many Black single mothers, this is what the struggle is about."

Because many families headed by single women are poor, they frequently must turn to welfare to survive. The amount of financial support available to welfare recipients in most states barely allowed families to make ends meet. In a recent study of welfare in the 1980s, for example, one researcher met a divorced mother of two whose combined cash aid and food stamps amounted to a mere $12 per day. "This is probably about the lowest point in my life," she admitted, "and I hope I never reach it again. Because this is where you're just up against a wall. You can't make a move. You can't buy anything that you want for your home. You can't go on vacation. You can't take a weekend off and go see things because it costs too much." The stigma attached to welfare made matters worse. Using food stamps—government issued coupons with which recipients buy food items—often brought stares and whispers of disgust from clerks and consumers standing by. "It's absolutely blatant in stores," reported one woman interviewed in the early 1980s. "They'll smile and be chatting with you, and then they see you pull out the food stamps— they just freeze up. And they scrutinize the food." This kind of behavior toward welfare recipients took its toll on children as well. One black single mother remembered when her daughter refused to participate in the free lunch program at school. "So I had to scrape for the last couple of years while she was in middle school and try to make ends meet so that I could send her with a dollar or two dollars every day. Which is a big chunk out of our budget. The food program at school is a big help. But rather than see her mistreated, or have her friends sit away from her, this is what I had to do."

The majority of single black mothers who received welfare during the 1980s, however, did so for an average of only six months, and most had to supplement aid with odd jobs in order to make ends meet. Be-

U.S. DEPARTMENT OF AGRICULTURE
FOOD COUPON
E00485260P
DO NOT FOLD OR SPINDLE

J

VALUE
1
DOLLAR

SERIES 1992 B

DECLARATION OF INDEPENDENCE

NON-TRANSFERABLE
EXCEPT UNDER CONDITIONS PRESCRIBED BY THE SECRETARY OF AGRICULTURE

D3   351

A food stamp good for $1 worth of food.

sides, not all poor African Americans received public assistance, nor were they the primary beneficiaries of welfare. In 1991, 61% of all persons on welfare were white. Blacks, by comparison, made up only 33% of welfare recipients. And many who did qualify for some form of public assistance did not always receive it. A 1979 study revealed that 70 percent of all unemployed blacks never received any unemployment benefits; more than half of all poor black households received no AFDC or General Assistance; half of all black welfare households received no Medicaid coverage and 58 percent of all poor black households received benefits from only one or two of the seven income programs available to assist the poor. There are many reasons why a substantial number of poor people did not receive full benefits. In some cases, the lengthy application process discouraged applicants; in other instances, computer errors, misplaced files, or unsympathetic or ill-informed case workers were to blame. But in many cases, black men and women living below the poverty line were simply too proud to accept welfare.

CHAPTER 4

LIVING THE DREAM?
THE BLACK MIDDLE CLASS

◇ ◇ ◇

With the dismantling of segregation, many upwardly mobile black families moved to the suburbs hoping to find the idyllic lifestyle associated with suburban home ownership. Some found it, but they also often found hostile or indifferent white neighbors, racist police officers, and a sense of isolation from other African Americans.

To the residents of Philadelphia, July 1976 must have felt like the hottest month in that city's history. Throngs of people from all over the country and throughout the world invaded the "City of Brotherly Love" to celebrate the 200th birthday of the Declaration of Independence. Waving overpriced flags and wearing red, white, and blue outfits, they came to examine the famous crack in the Liberty Bell and see firsthand the document that announced the beginning of this country's democratic journey.

In the neighborhoods just north, west, and south of the celebrations, a growing number of jobless and working-poor African Americans were fighting just to survive. Like other cities across the country, Philadelphia had been hit by recessions that left many African Americans unemployed, applying for welfare, or taking whatever jobs they could get in the service sector.

While the patriotic celebrations of the moment cast a shadow over Philadelphia's dark ghettos, hiding much of the recent devastation that would characterize the next two decades, a group of African-American leaders was trying to get the bicentennial committee to acknowledge the black presence in the past 200 years of history. The fact that the majority of Africans in America were still slaves when the Declaration of Independence was signed made many bicentennial organizers uncomfortable. Instead, they tried to integrate the celebrations by highlighting black

James McPhail, a teacher and restaurateur, poses proudly in his car while his family stands on the steps of their new home in Washington, D.C.

achievement in business, politics, the arts and entertainment, sciences, and education.

By emphasizing black achievement and paying less attention to the crumbling ghettos in earshot of the Liberty Bell, the organizers of the bicentennial were not being entirely dishonest. Just as the majority of African Americans experienced immense poverty, segregation, violence, and rising racism, some black professionals and entrepreneurs were reaping the fruits of integration. Of course, there had always been middle- and upper-class blacks, but in the past they succeeded in a segregated economy, lived in segregated neighborhoods, and had to operate in an atmosphere of outright racial discrimination. Although discrimination did not disappear entirely, the civil rights struggles of the previous two decades helped usher in affirmative action programs that gave minorities and women preference in hiring and college admission to compensate for past and present discrimination.

"We were all . . . children of the civil rights movement: the nation had changed its laws and, in some respects, its ways during our childhoods and adolescences. We were living the opportunities for which generations of black folk had fought and died. Walking paths wet with the blood of our martyrs, we felt an uneasy fear that taking advantage of those opportunities was changing us."

These words were written in 1991 by Yale law professor and best-selling author Stephen L. Carter. Carter exemplifies what it meant for a generation of young people to live the American Dream. A graduate of Yale Law School, Carter turned out to be a gifted legal scholar and talented writer. In another era, a black person of his considerable talents might not have had the chance to attend Yale or to accept a major professorship at his alma mater. But affirmative action policies and an aggressive recruitment effort to attract African Americans to the school opened doors for him that had been closed to previous generations. He is clearly one of those who "made it." Between his salaries, royalties on his book sales, and fees for speaking engagements, Professor Carter makes more than enough money to live a comfortable middle- or upper-middle-class existence.

And yet, Carter is somewhat ambivalent about how his success and the particular road he had to take to achieve it has changed him and other black professionals. Everywhere he turned, his white colleagues hinted that he did not make it on his own merit; that every college and every law firm opened doors to him because he was black, not because he was good. Some days he believed this argument. Other days he felt enraged that so many of his colleagues viewed him as the representative of a race rather than as an individual. Occasionally he convinced himself that his success was entirely the result of his own initiative and hard work. Indeed, there were moments when Carter believed that the old racial barriers of the past had been completely destroyed. But just when life seemed good, the handsomely attired and articulate scholar would be reminded of his race. "When in New York, for example, if I am traveling with a white person, I frequently swallow my pride and allow my companion to summon the taxi as I hang back—for to stand up for my rights and raise the arm myself would buy only a tired arm and no ride. For a black male, blue jeans in New York are a guaran-

Black cartoonist Ollie Harrington pokes fun at the racist attitudes encountered by African Americans in all walks of life.

by Ollie Harrington

"Doctor Jenkins, before you read us your paper on inter-stellar gravitational tensions in thermo-nuclear propulsion, would you sing us a good old spiritual?"

tee of ill-treatment. There are the jewelry-store buzzers that will not ring, the counter clerks who will not say 'Sir,' the men's departments with no staff to be found."

Carter's mixed feelings about his success are characteristic of a rapidly expanding class of black urban and suburban professionals who came of age during the 1950s and 1960s. Their numbers increased substantially during the 1970s. In 1970, 15.7 percent of black families had incomes over $35,000; by 1986 the percentage had grown to 21.2 percent. Likewise, black families earning more than $50,000 almost doubled, increasing from 4.7 percent in 1970 to 8.8 percent in 1986. And like Carter, their rapid success can be partially attributed to antidiscrimination laws and affirmative action programs first established in the 1960s and expanded under President Jimmy Carter during the mid- to late-1970s.

The roots of recent affirmative action policies can be traced to the Civil Rights Act of 1964. This important piece of legislation was largely a concession to the civil rights movement after nearly a decade of nonviolent activism in the South that culminated in the March on Washington in 1963. In particular, Title VII of the act outlawed employment discrimination. It applied not only to governmental and nongovernmental employers but to labor unions and employment agencies as well. Workers who believed they were unfairly discriminated against in the workplace or dismissed or not hired because of their race, sex, creed, color, or religion could file a complaint under Title VII with the Equal Employment Opportunity Commission (EEOC) or the Office of Federal Contract Compliance (OFCC). Both of these agencies were created to monitor employment discrimination and enforce the law. Unfortunately, the staff at the EEOC and the OFCC was small relative to the number of cases it received each year.

While lack of personnel within these institutions has led to a huge backlog of cases and limited their effectiveness, the EEOC, especially, has put pressure on firms to hire more women and minorities. For example, in 1973 the EEOC successfully sued the U.S. Steel Corporation for failing to promote black workers at its Fairfield, Alabama, plant. The court ordered U.S. Steel to expand job opportunities for its African-American workers. The EEOC discovered blatant incidents of white workers with less seniority being promoted to better jobs—mainly skilled machinist, clerical, technical, and managerial occupations. The court

An apprentice steel-worker (right) receives on-the-job training from a more experienced worker.

ruling required equal hiring of black and white apprentices and black and white clerical and technical employees until African Americans held about a quarter of these jobs.

Soon thereafter, the Detroit Edison Company was fined $4 million in punitive damages for discriminating against African-American employees, and a Detroit union local of the Utility Workers of America (UWA) was slapped with a $250,000 fine. The suit was initiated by a group of black Detroit Edison workers after the UWA and the International Brotherhood of Electrical Workers refused to file their grievance for them. Their primary complaint was that Detroit Edison employed very few black workers, turned down a large number of qualified black applicants, and kept blacks in the lowest-paid jobs. The judge in the case ordered the company to increase the proportion of black employees from 8 percent to 30 percent and to set hiring requirements that would ultimately place more black workers in higher-paying jobs with more authority.

Affirmative action policies were also responsible for briefly increasing black enrollment at major colleges and universities from the late-1960s to the late-1970s. Black enrollment rates rose from 27 percent in 1972 to 34 percent in 1976, before dropping steadily during the next decade. Many leading black scholars and corporate leaders who came of age in the 1950s and 1960s benefited from affirmative action initiatives. Because such policies were more strongly enforced at the federal, state, and municipal levels, African Americans employed in the public sector gained the most. By 1970, 28 percent of all employed African Americans held government jobs, and approximately 60 percent of all black professional workers were employed by governmental bodies. This is particularly striking when we consider that in 1970 African Americans held only 1 percent of the managerial and administrative jobs in manufacturing. Thus, the expansion of public sector jobs for minorities has been largely responsible for the growth of the black middle class.

However, the inclusion of African Americans in public sector jobs and managerial positions did not always translate into big salary increases. Many black families reporting middle-class incomes were often the result of two parents working full-time for fairly low or moderate wages. Besides, in 1979, 18 percent of all black female managers and 13 percent of all black male managers actually earned wages below the poverty line. Many middle-class black families who had purchased suburban homes during the 1970s lived from paycheck to paycheck; one layoff could mean the loss of their home. In fact, all economic indicators show that middle-class blacks, on average, possess substantially less "wealth" than middle-class whites who earn the same income. By wealth we mean total assets (savings, money invested in buying a home, stocks, bonds, retirement accounts, etc.) minus total debts.

James E. Hurt, a St. Louis businessman, was the first black Volkswagen dealer in the world.

Much of African-American wealth is concentrated in the hands of independent entrepreneurs, some of whom also benefited from affirmative action initiatives to provide more minority firms with government contracts and loans. The purpose of such programs was not to provide a handout to struggling businesses. Rather, they sought to rectify policies that had kept minority firms from obtaining government contracts in the first place and to improve the economic status

of all African Americans by establishing a strong foundation for "black capitalism." The Nixon administration, for example, created several subsidy programs to assist black businesses, including the Office of Minority Business Enterprise, the Manpower Development and Training Program, and the Minority Enterprise Small Business Investment Company. Although these programs might have been effective if properly funded, they were never given much of a chance: after Ronald Reagan was elected President in 1980 virtually all of these programs were cut back.

Between 1972 and 1977, the number of black-owned firms and their proportion of total industry revenue declined for the most part. The number of black-owned auto dealerships fell by 24 percent; black-owned hotel and lodging facilities dropped by 21 percent; and the number of food and eating establishments declined by 10 percent. In 1977, black-owned firms made up only 3 percent of all businesses in the country. By 1980, more than 80 percent of all black-owned firms did not have a single paid employee aside from the owner, and at least one-third of these firms failed within 12 months of opening.

Competition with other businesses only partly explains the failure of certain black-owned ventures. Black entrepreneurs have had more difficulty securing loans for their businesses than their white counterparts. A recent survey of 500 black entrepreneurs with an annual revenue of $100,000 or more revealed that 90 percent had been turned down by banks when they applied for business loans. Of those surveyed, 70 percent had to rely on personal savings to finance their business. Often, black business people have to turn to black-owned community banks for help. As the president of one such bank explained in an interview, "I've seen some attitudes . . . within the financial community toward minority entrepreneurs . . . saying that they have no skills, they have no ability to manage, or to borrow and successfully use those

Naomi Sims, the first black model to appear on the cover of Life *magazine, started her own skin care and cosmetics company designed specifically for the black market.*

borrowed funds. I've seen people who've been turned away from financial institutions, who've come to us, and we've helped them. And I cannot understand why those commercial banks or savings and loans haven't helped them."

Not all black business suffered during the 1970s recessions and Reagan-era cutbacks. On the contrary, the last two decades are filled with remarkable stories of black entrepreneurship. One rising corporate star during the 1970s was Naomi Sims, a high-fashion model originally from Oxford, Mississippi. After earning a degree in psychology from New York University and studying at the Fashion Institute of Technology, Sims quickly emerged as one of the most popular black women models in the country, making several magazine-cover and television appearances. In 1973, she helped develop a new fiber for a line of wigs and founded the Naomi Sims Collection, selling cosmetics and hair-care products nationwide. By 1977, her firm reported annual revenues of about $4 million.

By the time of his death in 1993, Reginald Lewis, the founder of the TLC Group, had amassed a fortune of more than $300 million, making him the wealthiest African American in U.S. history.

Reginald F. Lewis's road to success was a bit more traditional. Born in Baltimore, Maryland, Lewis was helped by affirmative action policies that enabled him to earn a law degree from Harvard in 1968. After working for one of New York's most prestigious corporate law firms, Lewis, with fellow attorney Charles Clarkson, started his own law firm on Wall Street in 1970. His firm helped minority-owned businesses obtain financing and structure deals. In 1983, Lewis launched the TLC Group, an aggressive investment firm with the specific purpose of acquiring companies. And acquire he did: in 1984 TLC bought McCall's Pattern Company (a manufacturer of sewing patterns) for $25 million—and sold it for $90 million three years later. Then in 1987, the TLC Group made history by purchasing BCI Holdings, the former international division of the Chicago-based Beatrice Foods. Comprised of 64 companies operating in 31 countries, BCI Holdings manufactured and distributed a wide range of food products, including ice cream, meats, chocolates, and soft drinks. Lewis's firm paid $985 million for BCI Holdings, making it the largest leveraged buyout of an overseas operation in the history of American business up to that time.

The year before Lewis's death in 1993, TLC Beatrice had revenues of $1.54 billion and Lewis himself had amassed assets of more than $300 million, making him the wealthiest African American in U.S. history.

Perhaps the best-known black millionaire is publishing magnate John H. Johnson, founder of *Ebony* and *Jet* magazines. Born in Arkansas in 1918, he migrated to Chicago with his mother at age 15. While working for the black-owned Supreme Liberty Life Insurance Company in 1942, 24-year-old Johnson decided to launch *Negro Digest*, a small magazine summarizing longer articles for and about African Americans. Raising the money was hard. "Most people had seen *Reader's Digest* and *Time*," he recalled, "but nobody had seen a successful black commercial magazine. And nobody was willing to risk a penny on a twenty-four-year-old insurance worker." That is, except for the Citizens Loan Corporation of Chicago, one of the few financial institutions willing to loan money to African Americans. They loaned him $500, but only after Johnson's mother offered to put up all of her new furniture as collateral. It was a good investment, for within eight months of its founding *Negro Digest* was selling 50,000 copies a month nationally. Three years later, Johnson launched *Ebony* magazine, a photo magazine modeled after *Life*. By 1991, the Johnson companies reported total gross sales of $252 million. According to *Forbes* magazine, Johnson headed one of the 400 richest families in the United States.

John H. Johnson, the founder of Ebony *and* Jet *magazines, headed a publishing empire that recorded total gross sales of $252 million in 1991.*

The combination of higher incomes and the dismantling of legal segregation enabled many rising middle-class black families to flee collapsing ghettos and move out to the suburbs or to lavish townhouses and brownstones in wealthy urban communities. The trend is reflected in the rapid suburbanization of the African-American population during the 1970s and 1980s: between 1970 and 1986, the black suburban population grew from 3.6 million to 7.1 million. Although they often left behind deteriorating neighborhoods, a growing drug economy, and a rapidly expanding army of unemployed men and women, most blacks could not escape bigotry. To their surprise, some middle-class black families who moved into predominantly white suburbs discovered burning crosses (a symbol of the Ku Klux Klan, a white supremacist group) on their lawns, hate mail, and letters from property owners' associations concerned that their presence would lower property values.

Potential black homebuyers also had to deal with real estate agents who deliberately steered them to poorer, predominantly black neighborhoods, and with financial institutions that blatantly discriminated against African Americans. The evidence of discrimination against African Americans in housing is overwhelming. Numerous studies conducted in major metropolitan areas since the 1960s demonstrated that real estate agents frequently showed black home buyers different properties, withheld information, or simply lied about the status of the property in question. This practice of steering black home buyers toward nonwhite neighborhoods is a form of discrimination known as "redlining." Similarly, a massive study of 10 million applications to savings and loan associations between 1983 and 1988 revealed that the rejection rate for blacks applying for home mortgages was more than twice that of whites, and that high-income African Americans were rejected more than low-income whites.

What is clear from such stories of discrimination is that the dismantling of legal barriers to segregation has not been completely effective. Indeed, by some measures racial segregation has increased in the urban North during the last three decades. Despite evidence that middle- and upper-income African Americans were the greatest beneficiaries of integration, it is interesting to note that in some major cities African Americans earning more than $50,000 were as segregated as those making less than $2,500 annually. Of course, in a few cases middle-class blacks have chosen predominantly black suburban enclaves in well-to-do communities such as Prince Georges County, Maryland (just outside of Washington, D.C.), or sections of Westchester County, a community north of New York City. Their decision is understandable given the history of violence and discrimination directed at African Americans who try to integrate all-white suburban communities. But fear of racist attacks and the desire for respectful neighbors indicate the narrowness of choices that are offered to blacks compared to whites.

School integration, another component of African Americans' desire to reach for the American Dream, quickly became one of the most contested racial battlefields during the post–civil rights era. A quarter of a century after the landmark case of *Brown* v. *Board of Education of Topeka, Kansas* (1954), in which the Supreme Court ruled that segregation in public education was unconstitutional, the nation's public schools looked as segregated as they had ever been. Although black children made up about one-fifth of the total public school enrollment, almost two-thirds went to schools with at least 50 percent minority enrollment. This pattern is even more striking in major cities, where African-American children attended underfunded public schools while many white students, often the children of urban professionals, have deserted the public school system for private institutions. By 1980, for example, whites made up only 4 percent of public school enrollment in Washington, D.C., 8 percent in Atlanta, 9 percent in Newark, and 12 percent in Detroit.

Drastic measures were needed to remedy this situation, especially since middle-class families who had migrated to the suburbs took precious tax dollars needed to run city schools. With fewer well-paid, property-owning families living in urban areas, the property taxes so essential to funding education and other city services declined considerably. Under pressure from black families who wanted to send their children to better-funded schools in the suburbs and civil rights groups that believed the nation should live up to the *Brown* decision, school boards across the country tried to achieve racial balance by busing students to schools in different neighborhoods.

The nation was sharply divided over the issue of busing. President Nixon vehemently opposed court-ordered busing, officials in the Department of Health, Education and Welfare thought it was a good idea, and the Supreme Court remained unsure whether it was constitutional or not. The clearest expression of resistance to mandatory busing came from white parents who believed the addition of black children from the inner city would bring down the quality of education. Indeed, in some

A group of white Boston parents gathers in front of the state capitol to voice their disapproval of a state plan calling for mandatory school busing.

cities busing programs were met with militant protests that frequently led to violence. Throughout the early to mid-1970s, organized resistance erupted in cities throughout the country, including Pontiac, Michigan; Louisville, Kentucky; Pasadena, California; and Kansas City, Missouri. The best-known clashes were in Boston, where most public schools had been racially segregated until an NAACP-led campaign won a court order in 1975 to bus children from predominantly black and poor Roxbury to Charlestown, a largely working-class Irish community. Over the course of the next three years, Boston police were called in to protect black children from white mobs screaming racial epithets and occasionally throwing bricks and fists.

The Boston busing controversy died down by the early 1980s, partly because liberal black and white politicians created a coalition that elected more supporters of integration to the city council and to the Board of Education. Besides, proponents of school integration could hardly claim a victory. By 1980, white flight to the suburbs and a decrease in the use of busing by conservative judges caused a resegregation of most big city school systems.

In the area of higher education, the backlash against affirmative action policies and financial aid for minorities took on many forms. During the late 1970s and through the 1980s, the number of reported racial assaults and acts of intimidation against blacks on college campuses showed a marked increase. The specific cases are chilling.

At Wesleyan University in 1981, black students found racist graffiti and flyers riddled with epithets and threats, including a leaflet advertising a fraternity "dedicated to wiping all goddamned niggers off the face of the earth." Ten years later, a white sorority at the University of Alabama hosted a party at which pledges painted their faces black and dressed as pregnant welfare mothers. Usually white backlash is much more subtle. One black college administrator vividly described the attitudes of white freshmen toward African Americans at his university: "Somebody will have the idea that the dorm is exclusively theirs, so therefore we can't have these 'germy, diseasey, dirty, filthy,' black kids live in their dormitory. . . . Black kids are seen as a gang now. They must be on drugs or crazy or something."

By far the most devastating form of white backlash in higher education was the partial dismantling of affirmative action initiatives. In the case of *Regents of the University of California* v. *Bakke* (1978), Allan

On April 5, 1976, a group of white high-school students opposed to busing traveled to Boston's City Hall to meet with a councilwoman who shared their views. Outside the building the youths attacked a black lawyer, Theodore Landsmark.

Bakke, an unsuccessful white applicant, claimed that he was discriminated against because the University of California, Davis, admitted African Americans with lower test scores than his in order to meet their quota of minority students. The Supreme Court ruled that Bakke had been unfairly denied admission to the medical school. The court did not overturn all forms of affirmative action, but it did argue that quotas—setting aside a specific number of slots for designated groups—were unconstitutional. The medical school's denial of admission to Bakke in order to increase the number of minority students was regarded by the court's majority opinion as "reverse discrimination."

Although Bakke won the case, the unspoken facts behind U.C. Davis's admissions policy call into question the court's opinion that he was a victim of reverse discrimination. First, the sons and daughters of influential white families—potential donors or friends of the dean of the Medical School—were also admitted over Bakke despite lower test scores. As had been the case historically, the dean controlled a handful of slots to admit special cases. Second, most minority applicants had higher scores than Bakke. This is an important fact, for the Bakke case left many observers with the incorrect impression that U.C. Davis admitted unqualified minorities. Most importantly, the decision was a major setback for efforts to achieve racial equality through social policy. Justice Thurgood Marshall, the first African American to serve on the Supreme

Court, dissented from the majority opinion. Marshall, who viewed the Bakke decision as a tragedy, did not believe that America was even close to becoming a color-blind society. "The dream of America as a great melting pot," he wrote in his dissenting opinion in the Bakke case, "has not been realized for the Negro; because of his skin color he never even made it into the pot."

Most African Americans who stood at the threshold of the Reagan era knew they had entered the worst of times. Equal opportunity, welfare, civil rights, and black power became bad words in the national vocabulary. Most white Americans believed they had given all they could give, and that any form of government support would be nothing more than a handout. A small but growing contingent of black conservatives agreed. And if this was not enough, the crumbling cities that African Americans and other minorities had inherited turned out not to be the utopia they had hoped for. They were dangerous, difficult places where racist police officers still roamed and well-paying jobs fled the city limits. Despite the rising number of black mayors, it became clear by the 1980s that a new freedom movement was needed.

CHAPTER 5

"HOW WE GONNA MAKE A BLACK NATION RISE?"

THE STRUGGLE FOR POLITICAL POWER

◇ ◇ ◇

In December 1979, Arthur McDuffie, a 33-year-old black insurance executive, was beaten to death by police officers in Dade County, Florida. The police said he was driving recklessly and had resisted arrest, but eyewitnesses believed it was a clear-cut case of brutality. African Americans who had followed the case closely knew who the real criminals were, and McDuffie was not one of them. To everyone's shock and dismay, however, in May 1980 an all-white jury returned a not-guilty verdict for all of the officers involved. That night black Miami exploded. Many inhabitants of the predominantly black and poor communities of Liberty City, Brownsville, Overton, and Coconut Grove took to the streets—turning over cars, setting fire to buildings, looting, throwing rocks and bottles at police and National Guardsmen. When the smoke cleared, Miami's losses exceeded $250 million; at least 400 people were injured and several were killed; more than 1,250 were arrested; and a 52-square-mile area of Dade County was placed under curfew from 8:00 P.M. to 6:00 A.M.

On closer inspection, it is clear that the Miami rebellion was not just a spontaneous response to an unfair verdict. It was a product of black frustrations caused by joblessness, economic deprivation, and immigration policies that clearly favored white Cubans over black Haitians, added to a string of incidents of police brutality and racial harassment that had gone unchecked during the 1970s prior to McDuffie's death. It also marked the most dramatic example of the growing feeling of politi-

In May 1980, riots erupted in Miami after a jury found four policemen not guilty in the beating death of a prominent black businessman. Members of the Florida National Guard stand watch outside a looted store.

71

cal powerlessness among poor and working-class African Americans. In an age when the number of black elected officials had increased dramatically and civil rights leaders achieved tremendous influence in national policy-making, Miami's black rebels displayed distrust toward their "leaders." When Andrew Young, former U.N. ambassador under President Carter and veteran civil rights leader, attempted to talk to black youths, he was shunned. As historian and social activist Manning Marable put it, "History and black people had pushed their so-called leaders aside."

The Miami uprising and the failure of black leadership was just a foreshadowing of the dark days yet to come. Throughout the country,

Smoke from burning buildings fills the skies of Miami after the Liberty City race riots. The Florida National Guard dispatched 3,800 troops to quell the uprising.

African Americans had become the most likely victims of police violence. According to one study, African Americans constituted 46 percent of people killed by police in 1975. By the end of the 1970s, police killings and nonlethal acts of brutality emerged as a central political issue among African Americans.

Racist violence was clearly on the rise in the 1980s. The number of racially motivated assaults rose dramatically, many of them on college campuses. Between 1982 and 1989, the number of hate crimes reported annually in the United States grew threefold.

Other signs pointing to a resurgence of racism in the 1980s include the proliferation of white supremacist organizations such as the Ku Klux Klan. By the late 1970s the Klan had tripled its membership and waged a nationwide campaign of intimidation against African Americans. In 1978–79, Klansmen initiated a reign of terror against black people, which included the firebombing of homes, churches, and schools in more than 100 towns and rural areas, and drive-by shootings into the homes of NAACP leaders. Very few of these incidents led to convictions. The Klan and other white supremacist organizations also gained influence in electoral politics. In 1980 Tom Metzger, the "Grand Dragon" of the Ku Klux Klan, garnered enough votes to win the Democratic primary in Southern California's 43rd congressional district. Similarly, David Duke, former Klansman and founder of the National Association for the Advancement of White People, was elected to the Louisiana House of Representatives.

David Duke, former Grand Wizard of the Ku Klux Klan, left the Klan to form the National Association for the Advancement of White People (NAAWP). He claimed that whites were being victimized by programs such as affirmative action.

Although racists like Duke and Metzger were in the minority, their electoral wins signaled a changed mood in the 1980s in the United States toward African Americans and other racial minorities. A new conservative movement emerged that strongly opposed affirmative action, immigration, and welfare. Even if this so-called "New Right" did not condone the resurgence of racism in the United States, its policies ultimately had a negative impact on African Americans. In particular, the election of former California governor Ronald Reagan to the White House in 1980 had disastrous consequences for black Americans, especially the poor. Reagan was a staunch believer in the "trickle down" economic theory—the idea that building big business would benefit everyone because its profits would somehow "trickle down" to the poor and middle class. With this philosophy as justification, the Reagan administration cut back social programs in favor of corporate investments and tax breaks to the wealthy. During his two terms in office, military spending increased by 46 percent while funding for housing was slashed by 77 percent and education by 70 percent. Money for Aid to Families with Dependent Children and the Food Stamp program, government programs that helped the poor, were also cut back substantially.

By the time Reagan began his second term in 1985, the living conditions of poor and working-class blacks were worse than they had been at the height of the 1973–75 recession. In 1985, about one out of every three African Americans, most of whom were women and children, lived below the poverty line, and the official black unemployment rates hovered around 15 percent nation-wide. In midwestern cities such as Chicago, Detroit, and Milwaukee, the percentage of blacks without jobs ranged from 25 to 30 percent.

Reagan-era spending cuts were especially hard on cities, where the vast majority of African Americans lived. In addition to closing down the Neighborhood Self-Help and Planning Assistance program, which allotted $55 million to assist inner cities in 1981, aid to cities was reduced to a fraction of what it had been under President Nixon a decade earlier. City governments were forced to cut their budgets as well, leading to massive layoffs of low- and mid-level city workers. Because blacks held many of these government jobs, they were hardest hit by these cutbacks.

Most of the black mayors elected since the late 1960s inherited this new urban crisis. With shrinking tax revenues caused by tax revolts and the flight of the middle class to the suburbs and almost no support from the federal government, most big city black mayors sought out whoever had money—which often turned out to be real estate developers and investors interested in building downtown financial centers. Coleman Young in Detroit, Maynard Jackson and Andrew Young in Atlanta, Ernest Morial in New Orleans, Carl Stokes in Cleveland, W. Wilson Goode in Philadelphia, to name a few, all faced this dilemma.

Perhaps the most telling example of this problem occurred in Los Angeles under Mayor Tom Bradley, a former Los Angeles police officer who was elected to the city council in 1963 and mayor in 1973. During his 20-year tenure as mayor, from 1973 to 1993, Bradley promoted poli-

During the administration of President Ronald Reagan, funding for social programs designed to help the poor was substantially reduced.

cies that favored the development of the downtown business district at the expense of poor communities in South Central Los Angeles that put him in office.

Because of the shutdown during the late 1970s and 1980s of numerous steel and rubber plants that had employed many African Americans in these neighborhoods, in some ways the decline of South Central was beyond Bradley's control. Economic conditions in South Central deteriorated faster than in any other L.A. community. A 1982 report from the California legislature revealed that South Central neighborhoods experienced a 50 percent rise in unemployment while

An unemployed clerical worker reads through a brochure while waiting to file a claim at the Michigan unemployment office in Detroit.

purchasing power dropped by one-third. The 1982 median income for South Central L.A.'s residents was a paltry $5,900—that is, $2,500 below the median income for the black population *in the late 1970s.* Youths were the hardest hit. For all of Los Angeles County, the unemployment rate of black youth remained at about 45 percent.

Just when no one thought life in South Central Los Angeles could get any worse, crack cocaine entered the illegal drug scene in the mid-1980s. Crack, or "rock," was a cheap, highly addictive version of powder cocaine that is smoked rather than inhaled through the nose. When this new drug hit the streets, it had an immediate and devastating impact on South Central Los Angeles as well as on other inner-city communities across the country. During 1984–85, emergency room admissions for cocaine trauma doubled and the number of juvenile arrests for drug dealing and related crimes increased fivefold. Violence also intensified as old gangs and new groups of peddlers battled for control of the crack market.

Two gang members in South Central Los Angeles. During the mid-1980s, gang violence increased as rival gangs fought to control the illegal drug trade.

In spite of the violence, the constant threat of arrest, and the devastating health crisis generated by the drug, for many black youngsters

selling crack was the only way to make a good income. Although the crack market might have put money into some people's pockets, for the majority it turned their neighborhoods into small war zones. Police helicopters, complex electronic surveillance, even small tanks armed with battering rams became increasingly familiar additions to the landscape of black Los Angeles. Housing projects were renovated along the lines of minimum security prisons and equipped with fortified fencing and mini-police stations. Some housing project residents were required to carry identity cards and visitors were routinely searched.

The intensive "law-and-order" policies of the Los Angeles Police Department were duplicated in most U.S. cities, with mixed results. Some black citizens complained that their communities were turning into police states. In Philadelphia, for example, police-civilian tensions escalated into one of the most brutal episodes of violence in at least a decade. After Wilson Goode was elected the first black mayor in Philadelphia's history in 1983, he immediately found himself caught between a white constituency who wanted a law-and-order mayor and a police force with a legacy of corruption and brutality. In fact, in 1986 a federal grand jury indicted seven Philadelphia police officers who had worked in the narcotics division for racketeering and extorting at least $400,000 plus quantities of cocaine from drug dealers.

But the key event was Goode's decision to allow the police to bomb the headquarters of a Black nationalist organization called MOVE in May of 1985. Located in a Philadelphia neighborhood called Powelton Village, MOVE was mostly a militant black back-to-nature movement that had attempted to create a rural, communal environment in the middle of the city. As a result of complaints from neighbors and MOVE members' hostile attitude toward police, mayor Frank Rizzo tried to root them out in 1978, culminating in a shoot-out that left one officer dead and several injured on both sides. In a similar standoff seven years

Mayor Wilson Goode's tenure as mayor of Philadelphia—he was the city's first black mayor—was marred by his decision to allow the police to drop a bomb on the headquarters of a black nationalist organization called MOVE. Eleven people, including five children, were killed in the blast.

later, Goode authorized the dropping of an aerial bomb which killed 11 people, including 5 children, destroyed 61 homes, and left 250 people homeless. The MOVE bombing marred Goode's administration and his relations with Philadelphia's black community until he left office in 1991. Perhaps the biggest blow to Goode's administration was that the commission appointed to investigate the bombing concluded that racism strongly influenced the actions of the Philadelphia police force. This was crystal clear from the first words spoken by Philadelphia Police Commissioner Gregore J. Sambor, who announced over the bullhorn at the beginning of the assault: "Attention MOVE! This is America!"

Increasingly, African Americans began to realize that putting a black person in the mayor's office was not enough to solve the problems facing black America. Unlike the days of the civil rights movement, when politics appeared to be clearly etched in black and white, the political landscape of the 1980s became more complicated. The appearance of a strong, vocal contingent of black pro-Reagan conservatives added to the confusion. Black conservatism was not new. The legacy of black conservatives advocating self-help and free market economics goes back at least to the mid-19th century. But during the Reagan years, black conservatives gained greater visibility in national politics and federal policy, distinguishing themselves for their advocacy of Reagan's "trickle down" theory and staunch opposition to affirmative action policies. (Ironically, most of these intellectuals had benefited from affirmative action in education and hiring.)

The most important spokesperson for this group, economist Thomas Sowell of the Hoover Institution at Stanford University, insisted that the problem of poor African Americans was one of values and the lack of a work ethic. He believed welfare and affirmative action policies undermined middle-class values of hard work and thrift and forced African Americans to become too dependent on government assistance. Black Harvard economist Glen Loury made similar arguments, insisting that racial preferences and equal opportunity legislation are worthless since the problems of the black poor are largely products of weak cultural values, broken families, and irresponsible parenting.

Thomas Sowell, one of the leading black conservative thinkers of the 1990s, believes that welfare and affirmative action programs are harmful to blacks, making them too dependent on the government.

While many African Americans agreed with aspects of what the black Right had to say, particularly its insistence on self-sufficiency and its critique of welfare, most rejected neo-conservatism as a strategy to solve the black community's problems. A 1982 public opinion survey revealed that 85 percent of African Americans opposed Reagan-era policies of cutting back social welfare programs. On the other hand, while most polls conducted in the 1980s indicated that African Americans supported increased government spending on the disadvantaged and endorsed affirmative action programs, they also revealed strong conservative views toward issues such as abortion and crime. Some African Americans, therefore, looked to political organizations and social movements that combined conservative social policy with racial militancy. The most potent example of this trend was the Nation of Islam (NOI), which grew dramatically during the 1980s.

The NOI had undergone a dramatic change after the death of Elijah Muhammad in 1975. As soon as Wallace D. Muhammad, Elijah's son, took over the leadership of the NOI, he denounced his father's earlier teachings that the white man was the devil and that white people

Under Minister Louis Farrakhan's leadership, the Nation of Islam has preached a fairly conservative message, focusing on self-help, the creation of black businesses, and maintaining traditional relations between men and women.

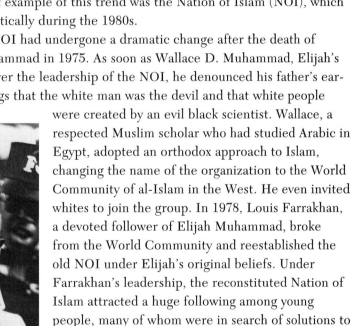

were created by an evil black scientist. Wallace, a respected Muslim scholar who had studied Arabic in Egypt, adopted an orthodox approach to Islam, changing the name of the organization to the World Community of al-Islam in the West. He even invited whites to join the group. In 1978, Louis Farrakhan, a devoted follower of Elijah Muhammad, broke from the World Community and reestablished the old NOI under Elijah's original beliefs. Under Farrakhan's leadership, the reconstituted Nation of Islam attracted a huge following among young people, many of whom were in search of solutions to joblessness, drug addiction, and the inability of poor African Americans to effect change in the political structure. Ironically, the Nation for the most part continued to distance itself from direct political participation and supported a fairly conservative agenda. Its policies centered on self-help, the creation of black business, and the maintenance of traditional relations between men and women.

The popularity of the NOI stems in part from its efforts to root out drug dealers from inner-city communities and its emphasis on community economic development. Through its economic wing, People Organized and Working for Economic Rebirth (POWER), the NOI has tried to create a nationwide cooperative of black businesses so that consumers and entrepreneurs can coordinate a massive "buy black" campaign. POWER has also introduced its own products, from soaps and shampoos to food items, which it markets through black stores or street corner vendors. By encouraging young, jobless African Americans to sell POWER products, they sought to create alternatives to crime and drug dealing and instill in them a sense of entrepreneurship.

Despite its conservative social policies and its tendency to stay out of electoral politics (an important exception being its support for Jesse Jackson's 1984 bid for the Presidency), the NOI is still regarded by many as an extremist organization. The Central Intelligence Agency (CIA) and the Reagan administration remained convinced that the NOI maintained ties to Arab terrorist organizations, especially after Libyan president Muammar Qaddafi extended a $5 million interest-free loan to the Nation to help start POWER. Furthermore, the NOI developed a reputation as a proponent of anti-Semitism because of several remarks made by Farrakhan and other NOI leaders. In 1983, for example, Farrakhan caused a national controversy when he described Nazi leader Adolf Hitler as "wickedly great." Although his point was to show how greatness could be used in the service of evil, the press reports interpreted Farrakhan's remark as praise for Hitler.

Although more radical black political activists rejected the NOI's conservatism, they agreed that African Americans needed to develop a road to political power independent of either the Democrats or the Republicans. Indeed, they had tried to build such a movement back in 1972, when the National Black Political Assembly first met in Gary, Indiana. But as more and more black elected officials became integrated into the Democratic party machine (and to a lesser extent, the Republican party), the idea of an independent road lost its appeal during the late 1970s. However, the failure of the Carter administration to respond to black needs, followed by the election of Reagan, compelled black political activists to reopen the discussion of an independent movement.

Thus in 1980, the National Black Independent Political Party (NBIPP) was formed to meet the challenge. Conceived as a democratic,

Shoppers at a Black Muslim supermarket in Washington, D.C, are presented with a variety of products from black-owned businesses, including Muslim Farm beef.

mass-based political movement capable of embracing a range of organizations and ideas without suppressing differences, NBIPP attracted between 1,500 and 2,000 delegates to its founding convention in November 1980. NBIPP's constitution called for strategies to work within the electoral arena and the development of community institutions that would involve ordinary people in local decision-making and ultimately shape public policy. Perhaps NBIPP's most revolutionary proposal was to put in place mechanisms that would ensure gender equality throughout the organization. Among other things, its charter and constitution called for equal gender representation in all leadership positions.

Unfortunately, NBIPP could not compete with the Democratic party, which continued to attract the vast majority of black voters. Nevertheless, it did set the stage for two historic political campaigns: Harold Washington's 1983 mayoral race in Chicago and Jesse Jackson's bid for President in 1984. Although both of these campaigns took place within the Democratic party, they can be characterized as "independent" since they drew more on grass-roots organizing than mainstream party support.

No one believed Harold Washington could win when he announced his candidacy for mayor in 1983. Chicago had never had a black mayor, and given its long history of racial animosity and its well-entrenched Democratic political machine in city hall as well as in Congress, a black challenger was viewed as a long shot. Chicago did not have a black majority, and the percentage of African Americans who went to the polls had not been very high. To win such an election, Washington would have to appeal to a significant proportion of white and Latino voters and convince hundreds of thousands of complacent, frustrated black adults to register and come out to the polls.

A veteran of Chicago politics and a native of the city, Harold Washington understood what he had to do. After earning a B.A. from Roosevelt University in 1949 and a J.D. from Northwestern University Law School in 1952, Washington worked as assistant city prosecutor in Chicago until he was able to establish his own private law practice. As a Democrat, Washington became a rising star in state politics, serving in

Chicago mayor Harold Washington at a press conference announcing funding for a community center in 1986. As Chicago's first black mayor, Washington struggled against the entrenched power structure, which had long denied access to blacks.

the state House of Representatives from 1965 to 1976 and the Illinois State Senate from 1977 to 1980. In 1980, campaigning on a progressive agenda of racial equality and justice for working people and the poor, Washington was elected to the U.S. House of Representatives.

By 1983, Washington felt the time had come to make a bid for mayor of Chicago. African Americans, in particular, were frustrated with the incumbent, Jane Byrne, whose policies did little to help the poor, provide jobs, or place blacks in appointed positions within city hall. In opposition to the Byrne administration, local black and Latino activists began to mobilize support for Washington's campaign. The movement not only waged successful voter registration campaigns, increasing the number of black voters by 180,000 in 1982, but enjoyed substantial support from liberal whites.

In a hotly contested primary election in which the white vote was split between Byrne and Richard M. Daley, the son of former mayor Richard Daley, Washington scored a narrow victory. Last-minute Byrne campaign propaganda played on the racial fears of Chicago's white voters, subtly warning that a black mayor would undermine white privilege. Such fears were made even more explicit in the general election, especially after Byrne briefly announced her intention to run as a write-in candidate in order to save a "fragile" city that, in her words, was "slipping." When Byrne realized this tactic would not work, however, she withdrew. Despite heightened racial tensions and a very nasty campaign, Washington also beat his Republican challenger, Robert Epton, in yet another close election.

Once in office, however, Washington soon discovered that he was a long way from "victory." Members of the city council tied to the old Chicago machine opposed virtually everything the Washington administration tried to do. Yet, in spite of this opposition, he created the Commission on Women's Affairs, successfully pushed for a state law giving public employees the right to form labor unions, and implemented affirmative action policies to increase the number of women and minorities in government.

Yet, like all big-city mayors, Washington faced problems beyond his control. The Chicago Police Department still had a reputation for brutality and terrorism against minorities. Big business was reluctant to increase investment in Chicago since Washington was labeled a radical and his ability to govern in opposition to the machine was constantly being questioned. Moreover, he spent much of his time trying to clean up generations of mismanagement, corruption, graft, and budget deficits. He was reelected in 1987, but his reform efforts came to a halt when he died of a heart attack soon after returning to work.

Meanwhile, as Harold Washington launched his historic campaign for mayor, a group of black activists—mainly independents, Democrats, and labor organizers—began debating the pros and cons of running an African American in the 1984 Presidential elections. Most agreed on the futility of running an independent, especially in light of NBIP's inability to become a powerful force in politics. Instead, they wanted to run someone within the Democratic party who could pressure mainstream white candidates to be more responsive to black needs. Black elected officials and other party supporters were afraid that the Democrats were promoting more conservative policies in order to attract white working-class voters who had voted for Reagan in 1980. A black candidate, it was argued, could not only show how valuable blacks were to the party but could run on a more liberal and even radical agenda. Such a candidate would not merely espouse racial justice and civil rights; rather, he or she would focus on workers' rights, the environment, nuclear disarmament, and issues affecting women, Latinos, Asian Americans, and gays and lesbians.

Few established black politicians in the early 1980s believed such a campaign could be anything but symbolic, and few were in the mood for symbolism. Even before a candidate was named, several African-American leaders opposed the plan.

However, one of the strongest supporters of a black Presidential candidate was Jesse Jackson. Because Jackson was so outspoken about the need to run a black candidate, he quickly emerged as the movement's spokesman. In no time, the media dubbed him the next Presidential candidate, a label Jackson himself did little to dispel. By the spring of 1983, opinion polls revealed that Jackson ranked third among the potential slate of Democratic candidates.

Jesse Jackson turned out to be an ideal choice. Born in Greenville, South Carolina, in 1941, he left South Carolina to attend the University of Illinois in 1959, hoping that life in the North would prove less humiliating than life in the segregated South. It wasn't true. Following several bouts with racism, he returned to the South to attend North Carolina Agricultural and Technical College, where he starred on the football

The Reverend Jesse Jackson's campaign for the Presidency in 1984 was not focused solely on issues concerning African Americans. He also championed the rights of women and labor and supported environmental causes. So many different groups were represented by his campaign that they became known as the Rainbow Coalition.

team and quickly emerged as a leader in the civil rights sit-ins in Greensboro, North Carolina. After earning a bachelor's degree in sociology, Jackson entered Chicago Theological Seminary, where he was ordained as a Baptist minister in 1968. An activist in the Southern Christian Leadership Conference since 1965, Jackson founded Operation PUSH (People United to Save Humanity) in 1971 in order to further the cause of human rights around the globe and to help the poor develop strategies to rise out of poverty.

Although Jackson was consistently described by the media as representing a "black agenda," his campaign and platform reflected the interests of many different groups. His staff included environmentalists, feminists, and labor organizers as well as black and Latino grassroots community activists. The campaign encompassed so many different issues and different ethnic groups that Jackson dubbed it the "Rainbow Coalition." Most importantly, Jackson brought to the Presidential race a vision for a new America that challenged politics as usual. In a speech before the Democratic National Convention in 1984, he issued the following challenge to a new generation of Americans:

> Young people, dream of a new value system. Dream of teachers, but teachers who will teach for life, not just for a living. Dream of doctors, but doctors who are more concerned with public health than personal wealth. Dream of lawyers, but lawyers who are more concerned with justice than a judgeship. . . . of authentic leaders who will mold public opinion against a headwind, not just ride the tailwinds of opinion polls.

In spite of Jackson's vision, support from mainstream black politicians within the Democratic party was slow in coming because many believed a vote for Jackson would undermine efforts to beat the incumbent, Ronald Reagan. Jackson also maintained strained relations with the Jewish community, partly because he supported the right of Palestinians in Israel to have a homeland and because he would not repudiate his

relationship with the Nation of Islam, especially NOI leader Louis Farrakhan. But the most damaging incident occurred with the publication of an anti-Semitic remark Jackson made in private, which virtually destroyed whatever Jewish support he had in 1984.

Despite these and other problems, Jackson ran a respectable campaign, winning several state primaries and caucuses and garnering 3.5 million popular votes. He lost the nomination to Walter Mondale (who was subsequently crushed by Ronald Reagan in a landslide election), but Jackson's Rainbow Coalition made some very important strides. Its massive voter registration drive brought hundreds of thousands of new voters—notably African Americans and Latinos—into the Democratic party. He also gave the struggle against apartheid in South Africa far more visibility than it had had before and sharply criticized U.S. military intervention in Central America and the Caribbean.

The Reverend Jesse Jackson addresses a crowd of supporters while campaigning for the Presidency in 1984. An ordained Baptist minister, Jackson was highly regarded as a powerful, inspirational speaker.

By the time the 1988 election rolled around, more and more Democrats had come to realize that Jackson was a serious candidate. In spite of several impressive showings in a number of states, he again lost the nomination—this time to Michael Dukakis, the governor of Massachusetts. Dukakis was in turn defeated by George Bush, Ronald Reagan's Vice President. In one of the most viciously race-tainted campaigns in U.S history, Bush attacked Dukakis as "soft on crime" because under Dukakis's administration in Massachusetts a black man named Willie Horton had been paroled from prison and subsequently committed a rape. The image of black men as criminal rapists out to violate white women was an old theme that tapped into the already heightened racial fears of white Americans. The infamous Willie Horton ads not only helped secure Bush's victory but proved once again the power of race to shape American politics.

CHAPTER 6

"ONE NATION UNDER A GROOVE"
AFRICAN-AMERICAN CULTURE SINCE 1970

◇ ◇ ◇

Afrika Bambaataa (front), pictured here with his group the Soul Sonic Force, was an early pioneer of rap music, integrating European electronic dance music with South Bronx hip-hop. He also founded the Zulu Nation in the 1970s—a politically conscious organization of rappers, break dancers, graffiti artists, and others associated with hip-hop culture.

As the 1970s opened, the cultural revolution born in the 1960s had reached its height then slowly sputtered out. Afros and dashikis—loose shirts made of bright African fabrics—were the style of the day. The music was called "soul," and James Brown was still the Godfather—even if his record sales had declined a bit from his peak years in the late 1960s. Even the "ghetto" was a place to be proud of, a place where pure "soul" could be found. By the end of the decade, however, things got to be a lot more complicated. As the language of soul and black power began to fade, black music crossed over to white listeners and more black faces appeared on television shows about family life.

As in virtually every previous era, African-American culture stood at the center of American life. But more than ever, this culture was extremely diverse, reflecting generational and class differences within black communities. In the late 20th century, there seemed to be less agreement about "how to be black" than at any other period since the first generation of African captives—with their many different cultural and linguistic backgrounds—arrived on these shores.

Black popular music in the 1970s is often described as "crossover" because it either adopted elements of other nonblack musical styles or was deliberately produced in a way that would attract white audiences. In a period when the sounds and scenes of urban rebellion slowly faded from the evening news, and when at least some sections of American society were becoming more and more racially integrated, the very idea of "crossover" seemed to be a fitting label. Of course, black popular music has always "crossed over"—from the popularity of jazz among urban whites in the 1920s to the irreverent sounds of Chuck Berry and Little Richard in the 1950s.

From 1968 to the early 1970s, one of the most revolutionary "crossover" bands was Sly and the Family Stone. The first major pop band to be integrated by race and sex, it combined the heavy-bass line associated with James Brown (also known as "funk" music) with rock to create a new sound that appealed to black and white audiences. The lyrics explored political themes, particularly in songs such as "Everyday People," "Thank You for Talkin' to Me Africa," and "Stand!"

An even more poignant example of a crossover musician is Jimi Hendrix, the Seattle-born master of the electric guitar. Although he died quite young in 1970, Hendrix paved the way for greater black involve-

Jimi Hendrix on stage in New York City on January 12, 1970. He was one of the first blacks to play heavy metal, and his style continues to influence guitarists today.

"Love to Love You Baby" (1975) by Donna Summer was one of the first disco songs to get heavy airplay on radio stations.

ment in heavy metal. A major figure in the heavy metal and psychedelic rock movements, Hendrix did not shy away from political themes; his instrumental version of "The Star Spangled Banner," which evoked powerful images of war, suffering, and anger within the United States, is still a classic example of late 1960s protest music.

As the militant mood of the late 1960s died down, and as black radio stations attracted more and more white listeners, black artists developed styles that reflected the changing times. The Philadelphia-based songwriting team of Kenny Gamble and Leon Huff gave birth to a new musical format known as "soft soul." Utilizing orchestral arrangements, lots of ballads, and a very smooth rhythmic pulse, they created a pop sound that quickly became popular in discotheques—dance clubs where records replaced live bands—across the country. Some of the more famous examples of the Gamble and Huff sound include Harold Melvin and the Blue Notes' "If You Don't Know Me By Now," and the O'Jays' "Love Train."

Disco had its roots in black and Latino dance music, and its strongest links were to the gay community. Indeed, the rise of disco coincided with the gay liberation movement and the push for open expressions of homosexuality. One of the most important places for "coming out" happened to be the multiracial underground dance clubs and ballroom dancing dance halls. These were places where performers such as Sylvester, a black gay disco singer, adopted feminine or "camp" stage presences much like Little Richard had done two decades before. The Village People, a multiracial group of gay men, made a big splash parodying macho culture and attitudes. While these performers made it big well beyond the gay community, lesser known artists who were even more explicit about their sexuality rarely got contracts with big record companies. In fact, the first major record label to release a disco song with an explicitly gay theme was Motown; in 1978 it recorded Carl Bean's "I Was Born This Way."

Initially, early disco artists did not get much air time on the radio, although their music was popular in the clubs. The first groups to cross over into radio include the Hues Corporation with "Rock the Boat" (1974) and the extremely popular Donna Summer tune, "Love to Love you Baby" (1975). As disco became more popular among whites, it also became "upscale" and trendier. New York disco clubs moved to expensive downtown locations that often refused to admit poor black and Puerto Rican youths. By the late 1970s, however, disco had become so much a part of the white mainstream that the media ultimately dubbed the Bee Gees, a British group, the kings of disco.

The irony for black artists and audiences was that, while black musicians were losing precious radio airplay to disco music performed by whites, all dance music began declining in popularity. As more and more radio stations specializing in heavy metal adopted anti-disco slogans, the fortunes of black performers declined considerably in the larger world of popular music. A telling case in point is Music Television, better known as MTV. Launched in 1981, when the disco craze was beginning to wane, MTV started out playing only rock music videos, which targeted MTV's main audience of suburban white youth. In 1983, only 16 of the 800 videos in rotation were by black artists—mainly performers like Prince, who had a large rock-fan following. MTV executives began to rethink their strategy after Michael Jackson released *Thriller*, which sold 33 million albums worldwide, and Prince released a succession of big-selling albums. It was the massive popularity of rap music, however, that compelled MTV to place more black artists in rotation. In the process, the corporate executives and marketing experts finally realized that their "target audience" was more diverse in both background and tastes than they had realized.

Meanwhile, as disco moved up from the underground and artists like Prince moved "crossover" music to still another level of sophistication, the African-American underground scene took on new dimensions. George Clinton revolutionized black music despite the fact that he had virtually no big sellers or Top 40 hits. Leading groups like Parliament and Funkadelic, Clinton expanded Sly Stone's fusion of rock and soul and built on James Brown's funk style to create music whose impact was still being felt two decades later. With albums such as *Maggot Brain, Chocolate City, America Eats Its Young,* and *One Nation Under a Groove,* the Parliament/Funkadelic family not only introduced a complex, improvisational style to pop music but retained a black nationalist edge that had all but disappeared in the mid-1970s.

Some of George Clinton's biggest followers could be found in the parks and school yards of New York, among poor African-American, West Indian, and Puerto Rican kids who were themselves at the forefront of a cultural revolution. Known to the world at large as hip-hop, this

During the early 1980s, Prince created a style that attracted fans of punk and heavy metal as well as soul and rhythm and blues. His appeal reached beyond urban black audiences to the white suburbs.

predominantly black and Latino youth culture included rap music, graffiti art, and break dancing, as well as the language and dress styles that have come to be associated with the hip-hop generation.

The oldest component of hip-hop culture is graffiti. Of course, wall writing goes back centuries, from political slogans and gang markings to romantic declarations. But the aerosol art movement was quite different. Calling themselves writers, graffiti artists, aerosol artists, and subterranean guerrilla artists, the kids who started this art form in the early 1970s came from a variety of different ethnic groups and neighborhoods throughout the city of New York. Subway trains provided the most popular canvases. Writers often "bombed" the interiors of trains with "tags"—quickly executed and highly stylized signatures, often made with fat markers rather than spray cans. Outside the trains they created "masterpieces," elaborate works of art carefully conceived and designed ahead of time. Incorporating logos and images borrowed from TV and comic books, stylistic signatures, and inventive lettering techniques—bubble letters, angular machine letters, and the very complex "wild style"—the best aerosol artists produced complicated compositions using a vast array of colors.

By expanding on the music of Sly Stone and James Brown, George Clinton and his bands, Funkadelic and Parliament, revolutionized black music, despite the fact that radio stations did not play his records widely.

By the late 1970s, the Metropolitan Transit Authority in New York City was spending $400,000 per year cleaning the trains and added 24 million dollars worth of ribbon wire fencing designed to ensnare and shred the body or object attempting to cross it. Ironically, while the MTA largely succeeded in keeping the trains graffiti-free, aerosol art exploded throughout other parts of the city and spread across the world during the 1980s and 1990s. Tags became commonplace in most cities and masterpieces continued to pop up on the sides of housing projects, school yards, abandoned buildings and plants, under bridges, and inside tunnels that service commuter trains.

Rap music is clearly the most enduring and profitable component of hip-hop culture. Although rap music as we know it originated in New York during the 1970s, it has a long prehistory in African-American culture that can be traced back to preaching, singing the blues, the rhyming styles of black radio DJs, and toasting (oral stories

The hands of this DJ are a blur as he works two turntables at a booth set up at Crenshaw Mall in South Central Los Angeles.

performed in rhyme that are usually humorous but often filled with explicit sex and violence). But what made hip-hop music unique was the technology: DJs and producers transformed oral traditions by adding electronic drum machines, turntables, mixers, and, later, digital samplers. (Sampling refers to the practice of incorporating portions of other records, or different sounds, into a new recording.)

Soon the parks, school yards, and underground clubs throughout New York were overrun with DJs. One important figure was Grandmaster Flash, who is credited with inventing "scratching" or back-cueing records on the turntable to create a new percussive sound. The DJs were followed by MCs (meaning "masters of ceremony," though they were much more than that) whose job was to keep the crowd moving and the parties "jumping." The early MCs often relied on call and response from the audience. A common phrase might be, "Just throw ya hands in the air / and wave 'em like ya just don't care / if your man has on clean underwear / somebody say 'oh yea.'" These simple party phrases became more complicated rhymes, and by the late 1970s MCs, or rappers, were as much a part of hip-hop music as the DJs themselves. By 1977, Harlem and the Bronx claimed several pioneering rap groups: Double Trouble, The Treacherous Three, The Funky Four Plus One, Grandmaster Flash and the Furious Five, and Afrika Bambaata and his various groups. However, the first commercial rap hit, "Rapper's Delight" by the Sugar Hill Gang, was not recorded until 1979.

Women had been part of the hip-hop underground from its origins. Some of the pioneering New York women rappers include Lady B, Sweet T, Lisa Lee, Sha Rock, the Mercedes Ladies, Sula, and Sequence. But popular women artists such as Sequence or Roxanne Shante were often treated as novelty groups instead of legitimate rappers, despite the fact that the first wave of women rappers displayed skills equal to the best of the male rappers. Because rap was portrayed as "the voice of the ghetto," the tough street culture associated with men, women were discriminated against by promoters who believed they could not sell many records. It was not until the appearance of Salt N' Pepa, and later MC Lyte and Queen Latifah, that women rappers gained legitimacy and respect. Like female MCs who came after and before them, they challenged the notion that boasting and profanity were distinctly "men's talk."

Although early rap artists were known for their humorous or boasting lyrics, groups such as Grandmaster Flash also recorded songs such as "White Lines" and "The Message" that critiqued contemporary racism, poverty, police brutality, and drug use. Out of that tradition emerged dozens of rap groups devoted to radical political themes, including Public Enemy, KRS-1, Brand Nubians, and the X-Clan. Other groups, such as the so-called "gangsta rappers" dominant on the West Coast, produced chilling stories of modern "bad men," tales of street life, police brutality, crime, and domination over women.

With the appearance of her debut album All Hail the Queen, *Queen Latifah established herself as one of the first female rappers to achieve success. Songs such as* "Ladies First" *and* "UNITY" *are sharply critical of male sexism while celebrating the power and strength of black women.*

Though not all rappers were driven by political and social themes, the use of profanity and sexually explicit lyrics pushed several rap groups into the center of controversy. In 1990, for instance, 2-Live Crew became a symbol for those who wanted to protect freedom of speech under the First Amendment after obscenity laws were vigorously enforced in several states to ban sale of their recordings as well as live performances. In 1993, several black community groups, led by the Reverend Calvin Butts of Abyssinian Baptist Church in New York and representatives of various African-American women's organizations, denounced "gangsta rap" for its offensive, violent, and sexist lyrics. The backlash against rap music, in fact, spurred congressional hearings to investigate the matter.

Despite these attacks, hip-hop was clearly a dominant force in American popular music by 1994. It had grown in several different directions and developed its own subgroups, incorporating elements of Jamaican reggae, jazz, punk rock, and heavy metal. What was once

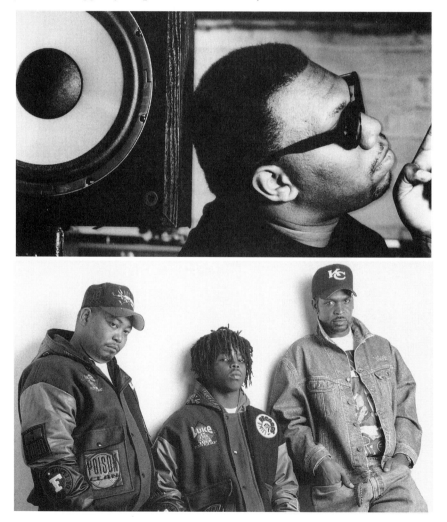

KRS-1 (top) and Luke Campbell (bottom right, a member of 2-Live Crew), were among the rappers who attracted controversy because of their radical or outrageous lyrics. In 1990, several states banned the sale of 2-Live Crew's albums because of their sexually explicit lyrics.

thought to be a passing fad has clearly secured a place in American cultural history.

Hip-hop might be the newest addition to the world of black music, but it is successful precisely because it draws on what came before. Jazz continued to be a mainstay in African-American culture, and its popularity seemed to have skyrocketed in the 1980s. Modern jazz experienced a kind of renaissance with the overnight success of trumpeter Wynton Marsalis and his brother, saxophonist Branford Marsalis, and the return of trumpeter and jazz pioneer Miles Davis (who had retired in 1975). Despite its renewed success, by the early 1990s the jazz world was sharply divided. On one side stood the "purists," strong advocates of more traditional jazz forms, or what is often called "repertory jazz." The strongest voice for the maintenance of tradition has been the Jazz at Lincoln Center Orchestra and the Smithsonian Jazz Masterpiece Ensemble. These ensembles highlight the music of major jazz composers, notably Louis Armstrong, Duke Ellington, and Thelonious Monk. On the other side stood musicians who experiment with "free jazz" or incorporate rock, funk, and hip-hop in their music. Their music might best be described as a "hybrid" or mixture of different musical genres. Greg Osby and Joshua Redman were among the more prominent young artists to fuse jazz and hip-hop, although some veterans, including vibist Roy Ayers, trumpeter Donald Byrd, and drummer Max Roach, had also moved in this direction.

Film and television has had a profound impact on race relations in the United States. In an age when segregation was becoming more entrenched, most Americans confronted black people through the big screen or their home television sets. The images of African Americans as violent, oversexed, lazy, and ignorant are as much a product of modern

In the 1980s, the success of trumpeter Wynton Marsalis led to a renaissance in modern jazz.

media as of old-fashioned racism. And yet, the same media can take
credit for breaking down old stereotypes, for changing our ideas about
history and creating a more complex image of what it means—or
meant—to be black in the United States.

In the early 1970s films about black ghetto life became extremely
popular among black and white audiences alike. Often called
"blaxploitation cinema," these films were less a response to black political radicalism of the era than the film industry's realization that
African-American consumers were a potentially profitable market, particularly in urban areas where white flight to the suburbs left inner city
theaters empty unless they catered to local audiences.

The signature film of that era was clearly Melvin Van Peebles's
Sweet Sweetback's Badasss Song (1971). Shot on a shoestring budget in
19 days, *Sweetback* quickly became the largest-grossing independent
production up to that point—an amazing accomplishment when we consider the fact that it was rated X. In this film, Van Peebles plays a regular
hustler whose bout with the police forces him to flee Los Angeles, always
staying one step ahead of the cops, vigilantes, and attack dogs. His flight,
assisted by ordinary community people, ultimately turns him into a rebel.
Despite the mass appeal in the black community, *Sweetback* was attacked by black and white critics alike, who called it degrading,
self-hating, and invidious.

What made *Sweetback* and films like it so popular to poor and
working-class black audiences? Van Peebles and such black filmmakers
as Gordon Parks, Sr., Gordon Parks, Jr., and Ivan Dixon generally focused on the lives of ghetto residents and emphasized racial pride,
community solidarity, and black power. No matter how stereotyped the
characters were, the people in "the streets" were constantly fighting back
and winning. The police and government were the source of corruption,
and even pimps, dope dealers, and petty criminals showed more morals
than white authority. One comes away from even the worst blaxploitation
film with a sense that a cohesive black community exists.

Not all dramatic films about African Americans were set in the
ghetto or emphasized violent revenge. *Sounder* (1972) was a "coming of
age" film set in the rural South. Starring Cicely Tyson, Paul Winfield,
and Kevin Hooks, it tells the story of a poor sharecropping family during
the 1930s struggling to make ends meet. Also noteworthy was the highly
acclaimed *Lady Sings the Blues* (1972), the moving story of jazz singer

Gordon Parks, Sr., a noted photographer and writer, was the first African American to direct full-length feature films for a major Hollywood studio. His best known films are Shaft *and* The Learning Tree.

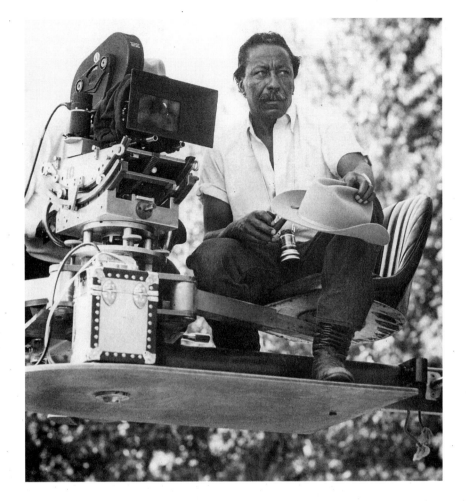

Billie Holiday's descent from being one of the most brilliant vocal stylists of the century to a heroin addict. And black cinema had its share of deeply sensitive love stories, such as *Claudine* and *Sparkle* (1976). Taken together, these films at least challenged the one-dimensional portrayal of African Americans created by the overload of blaxploitation cinema.

By the 1980s, as the number of black-oriented films declined, the possible range of roles actually widened. Now black characters—mainly men—had more supporting roles in films where their race was incidental. Roles written with white actors in mind, such as Lou Gossett, Jr.'s part as a Marine drill sergeant in *An Officer and a Gentleman,* created new opportunities for black actors to reach a wider audience. Actors such as Billy Dee Williams, Richard Pryor, Morgan Freeman, Eddie Murphy,

Denzel Washington, Alfre Woodard, and Whoopi Goldberg achieved superstardom in this new era. *A Soldier's Story* (1984), an intricate tale centering on the murder of an unpopular black army sergeant on a Louisiana military base during World War II, and *The Color Purple* (1985), a film about domestic violence, black male exploitation of black women, and lesbian encounters among black women, were two notable films of this era.

By the late 1980s Hollywood's relationship with black films shifted yet again. One cause of this change was the appearance in 1986 of Spike Lee, a young black independent filmmaker just out of New York University's film school whose first feature film turned out to be a box-office smash. *She's Gotta Have It* was a comedy about a young black woman's search for romance and sexual freedom in the 1980s and the three very different men to whom she was attracted.

The success of *She's Gotta Have It* and Lee's subsequent films did not suddenly compel Hollywood to take chances on young black filmmakers. What *did* make a difference was the rapid popularity of Hip Hop in American culture, which convinced advertisers and the film industry alike that there was big money to be made in the music and styles of black urban youth. Rap producers were called in to make soundtracks

The role of the tough marine drill sergeant played by Lou Gossett, Jr., in An Officer and a Gentleman *was originally written with a white actor in mind.*

The success of Spike Lee's first feature film, She's Gotta Have It *(1986), opened the door for other young, black directors, such as Mario Van Peebles and John Singleton.*

and the ghetto, once again, became the favored backdrop for a new wave of films. But unlike the blaxploitation films of the 1970s, the cult status of Spike Lee placed a greater premium on having young, black, and especially male directors.

Called by some critics the major example of the "new ghetto aesthetic," the film that opened up this new era was made by none other than Mario Van Peebles, the son of Melvin Van Peebles, whose *Sweet Sweetback's Badasss Song* had set in motion the blaxploitation era. *New Jack City* was not young Van Peebles' first film, but up to that point it was clearly his most successful, grossing over $40 million at the box office. In *New Jack City*, the story of the rise of a Harlem drug cartel and the crack cocaine industry it created, Van Peebles literally reverses his father's message of two decades before: in this story the black community is the problem and the police are the solution. The only black woman filmmaker to merit entrance into what otherwise is a boys' club of new directors was Leslie Harris, whose funny and gritty *Just Another Girl on the IRT* was underdistributed and largely ignored by the critics.

The blaxploitation film craze did not translate to television so easily. Attempts to turn blaxploitation films into TV serials, notably "Get Christie Love" (1974–75), "Shaft" (1973–74), and "Tenafly" (1973–74), were flops. "The Flip Wilson Show" (1970–74), the first popular black show of the decade, was created with white audiences in mind. Using a comedy/variety show format, Wilson often played characters that relied on common stereotypes of African Americans. Sitcoms popular during the 1970s, such as "Good Times," "What's Happenin'," "That's My Mama," and "Sanford and Son" focused on black working-class life, offering a slightly more sympathetic account of humor and perseverance in an age of rising unemployment, poverty, and violence.

The successful dramatic shows rarely appeared as serials. Rather, TV specials such as "The Autobiography of Miss Jane Pittman" (1974),

the personal saga of an elderly black woman who lived most of her life under segregation, and the miniseries "Roots" (1977) based on Alex Haley's historical novel tracing his family from slavery to freedom, captured the attention of broad television audiences.

However one TV series, "The Cosby Show," which premiered in 1984, dramatically changed black television. Against TV executives' assumptions, Bill Cosby created a black middle-class family free of old stereotypes, yet capable of entertaining millions of Americans of all ethnic and racial backgrounds. The show centered around Cosby, who played a congenial doctor named Cliff Huxtable, his five children, and his wife Claire, a successful attorney played by Phylicia Rashad. Though "The Cosby Show" was often criticized for ignoring race or painting too rosy a picture of black life, it subtly introduced issues such as the civil rights movement and apartheid in South Africa without making them central to the story. Moreover, given the then-dominant images of African Americans as an "underclass" with broken families, it is no accident that the show emphasized black middle-class success, a stable and unified black family, and high morals. And by dealing with universal issues, notably the problems of parenting, it invited audiences from different backgrounds to identify with the Huxtables.

For black writers and artists, "what is black?" has been a never-ending question. The post-1970 generation of fiction writers continued

"The Cosby Show" starring Bill Cosby was one of the most popular television programs of the 1980s. A sitcom about a happy, black, middle-class family, it diverged from television's usual portrayals of African Americans as poor and oppressed, or as ignorant buffoons.

to turn to African-American history for ideas, inspiration, and insights into contemporary issues they wished to explore in their art. But many more began recovering the dark side of black life—domestic violence, psychological trauma, the internal conflicts that rarely show up in heroic stories of black achievement. Others turned to satire, laughing at aspects of black culture and the absurdity of race.

Though this sort of self-criticism is hardly new to black literature, it became more visible in the post–civil rights era. Like most African Americans, black artists were products of a rapidly changing world in which defining one's culture or identity seemed more complicated than ever. An increasing number of middle-class African Americans raised their children in integrated settings. West Indians and Latinos of African descent, many of whom migrated to the United States after 1965, reminded other African Americans that all black people do not share the same ethnic heritage. Black gays and lesbians began to come out publicly, insisting on basic civil rights, respect and recognition for their sexual orientation, and a place in African-American history and culture. Black feminists grew increasingly vocal in African-American political, cultural, and intellectual life.

Partly an outgrowth of the resurgence of black feminism, black women writers such as Toni Cade Bambara, Rita Dove, Audre Lorde, Toni Morrison, Gloria Naylor, Ntozake Shange, Alice Walker, and Sherley Anne Williams brilliantly approached the subjects of sexism, domestic violence, and other forms of women's oppression. Through fiction, poetry, and political essays, these writers gave voice to the concerns and experiences of women, literally writing them into history. They challenged the trend among the previous generation of black nationalist writers to focus on men. And they revealed a complicated history of gender and family conflict that rarely found its way into history books, let alone African-American fiction.

In the process, these black women writers set new standards for creative writing. Gloria Naylor won the American Book Award for her first novel, *Women of Brewster Place* (1983); Ntozake Shange's highly acclaimed play, *For Colored Girls Who Have Considered Suicide/When the Rainbow is Enuf* (1976), received several awards, including the coveted Obie Award; Alice Walker's *The Color Purple* (1982) won both the American Book Award and the Pulitzer Prize.

Out of this generation of black women writers emerged one of the late 20th century's most celebrated novelists, Pulitzer Prize winner and Nobel Laureate Toni Morrison. Born Chloe Anthony Wofford in 1931, Morrison grew up in Lorain, Ohio. After earning a B.A. from Howard University and a master's degree in literature from Cornell University, she taught briefly at Texas Southern University in Houston and then returned to Howard University in 1957. In 1966 she left academia to become an editor at Random House, spending whatever free time she had on her fiction writing. *Beloved* (1987), her fifth novel, was a masterpiece—one of the most important literary achievements of the century. This beautifully written and very complicated novel about slavery, family life, and memory won the Pulitzer Prize for fiction. Throughout her writing, Morrison has turned to black culture and history as a way to explore the diversity of the human experience in the context of both love and hate, degradation and defiance, community and individualism. In 1993 she received the highest honor for her incredible achievements as a writer, artist, and intellectual—the Nobel Prize for Literature.

Since the 1970s and 1980s, several black writers have finally been recognized in genres in which African Americans have tended to be overlooked. By the early 1990s, for example, one of the country's most popular crime-detective novelists was black, Los Angeles author Walter Mosley. Each of the books in his trilogy, *White Butterfly, A Red Death,* and *Devil in a Blue Dress,* were instant successes. In the field of science fiction, Samuel Delany and Octavia Butler won major literary prizes for their work. They turned to the future rather than the past to explore issues of race, gender, and sexuality in contemporary society. Delany, a prolific author of 16 novels and novellas and at least five nonfiction books, twice won the coveted Nebula Award from the Science Fiction Writers of America. Octavia Butler published nine novels between 1976 and 1989, and her novella, *Bloodchild,* won both the Hugo Award and the Nebula Award in 1985. Her first series of novels actually linked the ancient African past to the future; its central characters include African healers, a 4,000-year-old Nubian "psychic vampire," and a variety of powerful, independent black women.

Toni Morrison, one of the 20th century's most celebrated novelists, was awarded the Nobel Prize for Literature in 1993. In her writing, Morrison uses black culture and history as a way to explore the diversity of the human experience.

In the world of visual arts, earlier generations of artists—collagist Romare Bearden, painters Jacob Lawrence, Elizabeth Catlett, Robert Colescott, and sculptor Martin Puryear—continued to have a huge influence on the American art scene throughout the 1970s and 1980s. More recently, a younger generation of black artists has deliberately broken with traditional conventions like painting and sculpture. Acclaimed sculptor David Hammons playfully used objects such as human hair, chicken parts, watermelon, and elephant dung to comment on racial stereotypes and African-American culture. Faith Ringgold, a Harlem-born painter and political activist, turned to the older "folk" tradition of quilting as her primary medium in the early 1980s. Adrian Piper has used photography, as well as drawings, texts, collage, and video technology, to bring out and thoroughly challenge her audience's racial fears and attitudes. A fair-skinned African-American woman who can sometimes "pass" as white, Piper made use of her own body to question people's assumptions about who is black and who is not.

Called by one critic "the post-soul era," black culture since the 1970s seems limitless in range and depth. Never before have there been so many different ways to be black, so much so that even those who mimic African-American culture have had a difficult time trying to decide what to copy. The history of black culture in the late 20th century is living proof that "blackness" has been—and will continue to be— multicultural.

CHAPTER 7

"AIN'T NO STOPPING US NOW"
BLACK POLITICS AT THE END OF THE CENTURY

◇ ◇ ◇

F or African Americans, the end of the 20th century looks very much like the end of the 19th century. The 1960s and 1970s, like the 1860s and 1870s, were decades of immense struggle and high expectations. Emancipation of sorts had been achieved and black communities looked to each other, and occasionally to the federal government, to help them secure their freedom. Most black people were optimistic. And they had a right to be, especially as they approached the 1990s. The successful mayoral bids by Michael White in Cleveland, Sharon Pratt Dixon in Washington, D.C., and David Dinkins in New York City were not only indicative of the growing political strength of African Americans in major metropolitan areas but proved that black politicians were capable of winning over large numbers of white voters. This was certainly the case with Douglas Wilder's historic election as governor of Virginia in 1989; he became the first African American elected governor of any state. The same can be said of the successful mayoral campaigns of Norman Rice in Seattle, the Reverend Emmanuel Cleaver in Kansas City, and Wellington Webb in Denver. In all three cities, the majority of voters were white.

Yet despite these impressive gains, in 1988 blacks comprised only 1.5 percent of all elected officials, more than half of whom served on local school boards or city or town councils. Moreover, in many other respects the situation for African Americans actually worsened. Aside from the economic disaster caused by the loss of decent-paying jobs,

A participant at the International Women's Year Conference in Houston in 1977.

reductions in social spending, and the decline in government subsidies to cities, racism and racist violence against African Americans actually intensified.

Perpetrators of racism were not simply a minority of deranged Klansmen. Since 1990, black customers and employees have filed suits against several nationally known restaurants for discrimination. In December 1991, for example, a group of black college students successfully sued an International House of Pancakes in Milwaukee, Wisconsin, for refusing to seat them. They were told that the restaurant was closed, though white customers were allowed in. The most notorious case involved Denny's restaurants. After the U.S. Department of Justice discovered a pattern of discrimination in the Denny's chain in 1993, Denny's corporate executives agreed to provide its employees with special training in nondiscriminatory behavior and to include more minorities in its advertising. Yet, in spite of these attempts to change its corporate behavior, Denny's continued to discriminate against black customers. In one striking case that led to a separate lawsuit, six black

Douglas Wilder, the first African American to be elected governor of any state, takes the oath of office to become the governor of Virginia in January 1990.

Secret Service agents patronizing a Denny's in Annapolis, Maryland, waited an hour for service while the white customers, including their fellow white agents, were served promptly. Other instances of discrimination frequently encountered by African Americans occur when shop owners refuse to open their doors to black customers.

Some of the Denny's employees who testified suggested that this kind of treatment of black customers was part of the company's rational efforts to reduce robberies and disruptive behavior. The fear of crime and the presumption that black people are more likely than whites to commit crime, regardless of their age or class background, has led retail outlets to adopt blatantly discriminatory measures. For example, in several cities, one must ring a buzzer in order to be admitted to certain stores during business hours. If the customer looks legitimate, the salesperson, manager, or security guard admits him or her. Not surprisingly, African-American patrons are frequently left outside to window shop. Patricia J. Williams, a nationally renowned African-American attorney and legal scholar, recalls one memorable bout with this kind of discrimination in 1986: "I was shopping in Soho [a neighborhood in downtown Manhattan] and saw in a store window a sweater that I wanted to buy for my mother. I pressed my round brown face to the window and my finger to the buzzer, seeking admittance. A narrow-eyed, white teenager wearing running shoes and feasting on bubble gum glared out, evaluating me for signs that would pit me against the limits of his social understanding. After about five seconds, he mouthed 'We're closed,' and blew pink rubber at me. It was two Saturdays before Christmas, at one o'clock in the afternoon; there were several white people in the store who appeared to be shopping for things for *their* mothers." The place in question was Benneton, an expensive clothing store known, ironically, for its ad campaign espousing tolerance and celebrating the breaking down of racial barriers.

Incidents like these, compounded by the impoverishment of a large segment of the black population, compelled African Americans to seriously question the costs and benefits of integration. This never-ending battle with white racism convinced some former advocates of integration to turn inward, to build separate black institutions. Others believed integration has failed precisely because the new generation of black youth did not have a sense of history and pride in their cultural heritage. They insisted that the perspectives and experiences of African Americans be represented in classrooms, boardrooms, and political arenas. They saw no contradiction in celebrating their African heritage and participating as equals in the white world.

Not surprisingly, black nationalism has made a comeback among the 90s generation—the sons and daughters of the 60s generation. The militant nationalist and Muslim leader Malcolm X emerged as the decade's central black hero. Kinte cloth (a colorful and intricately woven West African fabric), beads, and leather medallions with outlines of Africa became popular consumer items. On many college campuses more

This black entrepreneur in Detroit sells and wears Afrocentric clothes.

and more young people could be seen wearing dreadlocks (twists of hair worn long and uncombed) and sporting T-shirts bearing such slogans as "Black by Popular Demand" or "Black to the Future." Membership in the Nation of Islam and other black Muslim groups rose dramatically during the late 1980s and 1990s.

One important outgrowth of the upsurge in black nationalist sentiment has been the popularity of "Afrocentrism." Although there are many varieties of Afrocentric thought, the concept might best be described as a way of thinking and a type of scholarship that looks at the world from an African/African-American perspective. A good deal of Afrocentric scholarship argues that black people have a distinctive way of doing things, a set of cultural values and practices that are unique to their African heritage. Some scholars, such as Temple University professor Molefi Asante, locate the origins of this distinctive African culture in the ancient African civilization of Egypt, and offer prescriptions for maintaining this Afrocentric way of life. Some black educators and parents have called for the incorporation of an Afrocentric curriculum in public schools. Others have turned to independent schools emphasizing Afrocentrism. The number of such schools has grown dramatically during the 1980s and 1990s, particularly in major cities such as Detroit, Washington, D.C., Los Angeles, and Oakland.

Though Afrocentrism and varieties of black nationalism are associated with radicalism, these philosophies share much in common with those of conservatives. Molefi Asante, for example, has been sharply criticized for arguing that an Afrocentric life style includes distinct roles for men and women and that homosexuality is a form of deviance. In his words, homosexuality "is a deviation from Afrocentric thought, because it makes the person evaluate his own physical needs above the teachings of national consciousness." Black Christian conservatives agree. Organizations such as Project 21, Concerned Citizens for Traditional Family Values, and the Traditional Values Coalition, and publications such as the *Black Chronicle* have mobilized conservative African Americans to protest legislation that would protect gay and lesbian rights and to attack the NAACP and the National Urban League for defending the rights of homosexuals.

Black feminists too have been attacked by Afrocentrists, black nationalists, and black conservatives who have called for a return to traditional male-female roles and placed a good deal of blame for the

behavior of young black males squarely on the shoulders of single mothers, whom they characterize as irresponsible and incapable of disci-
plining their sons. One of the most controversial and best-known books
to attack African-American feminists was *The Blackman's Guide to
Understanding the Blackwoman* (1989). Written by a woman, Shahrazad
Ali, a formerly unknown black street vendor of Afrocentric products, this
vastly popular book caricatured black women as selfish, power-hungry,
aggressive, manipulating, and even dirty. Ali argued that true liberation
required that black women return to their traditional African roles as
child-care givers and supporters of black men.

The backlash against poor black women has had an even greater
impact on social policies. The image of poor black women as promiscuous, highly irresponsible single mothers who spend years and years
receiving welfare became increasingly popular in the late 1980s and
1990s. Although studies show that most women receive assistance for
very short periods of time as a transitional stage between jobs, and many
who do receive aid must nevertheless work part-time to make ends meet,
the image of welfare cheats and overweight, indulgent, lazy black mothers was far more common among white voters. It was so pervasive that
many liberal Democrats joined forces with Republicans to call for dramatic changes in public assistance. In fact, some of the most far-reaching
changes in social welfare were initiated after George Bush was defeated
by Democrat Bill Clinton in the 1992 Presidential race. Clinton's proposals included cutting welfare recipients off after two years and developing
mandatory "workfare" programs that require recipients to earn their aid.
Unfortunately, adequate daycare facilities necessary to enable single
mothers to work had not been developed as of 1994. And despite efforts
to create job training programs, the likelihood of landing a well-paying
job remained slim.

The simmering backlash against African-American women and the
efforts on the part of black feminists to reverse the trend were power-
fully dramatized by a single event: the confirmation of Supreme Court
Justice Clarence Thomas. A story of race, sex, and political intrigue, it
was perhaps the biggest media spectacle of 1991. What began as a fairly
routine and friendly hearing suddenly became a national scandal when
the Senate Judiciary Committee called University of Oklahoma law professor Anita Hill to testify. Hill had worked for Thomas when he was
with the Department of Education and later when he headed the Equal

Anita Hill testifies before the Senate Judiciary Committee in October 1991. Hill claimed that she had been sexually harassed by Clarence Thomas, a nominee for the Supreme Court.

Employment Opportunities Commission (EEOC). During the questioning, she revealed that Thomas had sexually harassed her—pestering her to go out on dates, bragging about his sexual prowess, and making explicit references to pornography.

Thomas's description of himself as a God-fearing, hard-working, self-made black man contrasted sharply with Hill's characterization of him as an avid consumer of pornography. Born in the little rural town of Pin Point, Georgia, he was raised by grandparents and attended Catholic schools most of his life. After earning a bachelor's degree from Holy Cross and a law degree from Yale University, he was hired as assistant attorney general for the state of Missouri in 1974, and in 1981 was appointed assistant secretary in the Office of Civil Rights in the Department of Education. In 1982 he accepted the chairmanship of the Equal Employment Opportunity Commission (EEOC), which he held until 1990. The Reagan administration chose Thomas for these two important posts precisely because he opposed affirmative action and had criticized established civil rights leadership. His leadership of the EEOC effectively weakened the commission's role in combating discrimination on the basis of race, age, and sex.

Thomas's appointment to the Supreme Court was especially important for African Americans because he was to replace retiring Justice Thurgood Marshall—the first African American to serve on the Court. The Congressional Black Caucus and several other black leaders outside of the government came out strongly against Thomas because of his lack of judicial and intellectual qualifications and his staunch conservatism. Though himself a beneficiary of Yale University's affirmative action initiative to recruit more minority law students, Thomas opposed affirmative action, supported cutbacks in social programs geared to help the poor, and consistently attacked civil rights leadership.

When the confirmation hearings began, most black voters knew very little about Thomas or his views. Many African Americans who backed the confirmation of Thomas, for example, did not know that his actions within the EEOC eroded black civil rights substantially.

Thomas's initial testimony and the White House press releases focused on his personal biography, emphasizing how he worked his way up from rural poverty to a successful career as an attorney and a judge. But lack of information is only part of the story. Many African Americans sided with Thomas simply because he was a black man about to hold one of the most powerful positions in the country. By emphasizing his impoverished rural upbringing he gained a sympathetic hearing from blacks eager to see a black man succeed. More importantly, he gained a sympathetic hearing from Democratic senators who were afraid to ask critical questions about his views on affirmative action and civil rights. Whenever these issues came up, Thomas would insist that he had an especially sensitive understanding of them because of his life as a black man from segregated Georgia.

During Clarence Thomas's confirmation hearings, many African Americans were torn between supporting Thomas, a black man who had risen from poverty to become a judge, and Anita Hill, a black law professor who accused Thomas of sexual harassment.

While Anita Hill's allegations could have disgraced Thomas and cost him the nomination, they actually worked in his favor. Many African Americans dismissed Professor Hill as a spurned lover or a black woman out to destroy a black man's career—a characterization not unlike Shahrazad Ali's bizarre assertion in *The Blackman's Guide to Understanding the Blackwoman* that black women sabotaged the upward mobility of black men. Tragically, the alleged victim of sexual harassment was turned into the villain. On the other hand, several polls and interviews reveal that a majority of African Americans believed both Thomas and Hill were victims of white racism. They believed that Hill was being used by the Senate committee to keep a black man from occupying one of the most powerful positions in the federal government. Thomas manipulated these underlying feelings by testifying before the Senate Judiciary Committee that the hearings were a "high tech lynching for uppity blacks who in any way deign to think for themselves." On October 16, 1991, the Senate voted 52–48 to confirm Clarence Thomas as an associate justice of the Supreme Court.

In spite of a high black approval rating for Thomas as measured by polls, many black people—especially women—were outraged by Thomas's confirmation. Several black feminist organizations and activist groups publicly criticized the appointment and used the hearings to draw attention to the issue of sexual harassment and the general backlash against women in the United States. Sixteen hundred black women signed a three-quarter page advertisement in *The New York Times* denouncing the appointment and explaining the significance of the hearings for black women. The ad highlighted the long history of racial and sexual abuse black women have had to endure, the lack of protection against such violations, and the perpetuation of stereotypes that continue to represent black women as sexually promiscuous and immoral. "We are particularly outraged," they said:

> by the racist and sexist treatment of Professor Anita Hill, an African-American woman who was maligned and castigated for daring to speak publicly of her own experience of sexual abuse. The malicious defamation of Professor Hill insulted all woman of African descent and sent a dangerous message to any woman who might contemplate a sexual harassment complaint.

Throughout the country, the Senate Judiciary Committee's behavior during the Hill-Thomas hearings sparked women's organizations to promote more women to run for public office. In 1992, more women ran for office than ever before, and the percentage of women who went to the polls rose markedly, representing 54 percent of the American electorate.

One woman inspired by the Hill-Thomas hearings to run for the U.S. Senate from the state of Illinois was Carol Moseley-Braun. Born in Chicago in 1947, Braun earned a bachelor's degree from the University of Illinois and a law degree from the University of Chicago in 1972. Upon graduation she worked as assistant U.S. attorney for the Northern District of Illinois, and later she won a seat in the Illinois state legislature and was elected Cook County recorder of deeds. Although she had very little money and an understaffed campaign team, Moseley-Braun beat incumbent Alan Dixon (who voted for Thomas's confirmation) in her 1992 U.S. Senate race, thereby becoming the first black woman to be elected to the U.S. Senate.

Though Moseley-Braun's election certainly benefited from women's response to the Hill-Thomas hearings, black women had already begun to have a greater presence in national politics in the late 1980s. Perhaps the most dynamic and uncompromising black elected official to emerge on the national scene in this period was California congresswoman Maxine Waters. Born one of 13 siblings in a housing project in St. Louis, Missouri, in 1938, she graduated from high school, got married, and took a number of low-paying jobs in order to make ends meet. She and her husband eventually moved to Los Angeles, where she worked in a garment factory and

In 1992, Carol Moseley-Braun of Illinois became the first black woman elected to the U.S. Senate and only the second African-American senator since Reconstruction. With barely enough money to buy one television commercial, the underfunded Moseley-Braun defeated the incumbent Alan Dixon and millionaire Al Hofeld in a hotly contested race.

then for the telephone company. In the late 1960s, Waters enrolled at California State University in Los Angeles, where she studied sociology, and then went on to teach in the Head Start program—a federally funded preschool program geared especially for poor and minority children.

Largely through her community work, Waters became involved in politics, winning a seat representing South Central Los Angeles in the state assembly in 1976. Her constant battles on the assembly floor produced some important pieces of legislation, including withdrawing investments of the California state pension fund from companies with ties to South Africa. Waters also established a vocational and education center in her district and increased access to social services for housing project residents in the Watts district. During this same period, she became active in national Democratic politics, serving as a key advisor to Jesse Jackson's 1984 Presidential campaign.

In 1990 Waters was elected to the U.S. Congress from the 29th district of California, becoming one of the most vocal African Americans in the House of Representatives. In 1991 she fought attempts to weaken laws requiring banks and savings and loans to service minority and low-income communities. In the aftermath of the riots that tore through Los Angeles in 1992, she emerged as the key spokeswoman for aggrieved residents of South Central Los Angeles. She and her staff organized residents of housing projects into carpools in order to get needed food, water, and other supplies that were unavailable during the uprising. Although she lamented the loss of life and destruction of property, she kept the issues surrounding the rebellion focused on the deteriorating social and economic conditions of African Americans and Latinos.

Not all significant political battles fought by African-American women took place in the sphere of electoral politics. Nor were they national in scope. Throughout the country poor, working-class, and some middle-class black women built and sustained community organizations that registered voters, patrolled the streets, challenged neighborhood drug dealers, and fought vigorously for improvements in housing, city services, health care, and public assistance. There was nothing new about black women taking the lead in community-based organizing. A century earlier, black women's clubs not only helped the less fortunate but played a key role in the political life of the African-American community. Even a generation earlier, when militant, predominantly male organizations like the Black Panther party and the Black Liberation Army

After her 1990 election to the U.S. House of Representatives, Maxine Waters became one of the most vocal African Americans in Congress. Here, with Jesse Jackson, she speaks to reporters after meeting with the U.S. attorney general to discuss the Rodney King case.

received a great deal of press, black women carried on the tradition of community-based organizing. If one looked only at South Central Los Angeles in the mid-1960s, one would find well over a dozen such organizations, including the Watts Women's Association, the Avalon-Carver Community Center, the Mothers of Watts Community Action Council, Mothers Anonymous, the Welfare Recipients Union, the Welfare Rights Organization, the Central City Community Mental Health Center, the Neighborhood Organizations of Watts, and the South Central Volunteer Bureau of Los Angeles.

Black women activists continued the tradition of community organizing, but in the 1980s and 1990s they confronted new problems. Of the new battlegrounds, one of the most important has been the fight against toxic dumping in poor black communities. Calling themselves the movement against environmental racism or, alternately, the movement for environmental justice, local African-American, Latino, and Native American groups, led largely by women, have fought against companies and government institutions responsible for placing landfills, hazardous waste sites, and chemical manufacturers dangerously close to low-income minority communities.

The evidence that poor African-American and other minority communities are singled out for toxic waste sites is overwhelming. One study released in 1987 estimated that three out of five African Americans live perilously close to abandoned toxic waste sites and hazardous commercial waste landfills. The study also revealed that the largest hazardous waste landfill in the country is located in Emelle, Alabama, whose population is 78.9 percent black, and that the greatest concentration of hazardous waste sites is in the mostly black and Latino south side of Chicago. A 1992 study concluded that polluters based in minority areas are treated less severely by government agencies than those in largely white communities. Also, according to the report, federally sponsored toxic cleanup programs take longer and are less thorough in minority neighborhoods.

The effects of these policies have been devastating. Cases of asthma and other respiratory diseases as well as cancer have been traced to toxic waste. Accidents involving the mishandling of hazardous chemicals have ravaged some poor black communities, often with little or no publicity.

The roots of the environmental justice movement go back to 1982, when black and Native American residents tried to block state authorities from building a chemical disposal site in Warren County, North Carolina. Since then, dozens of local movements have followed suit, including the Concerned Citizens of South Central (Los Angeles), and the North Richmond West County Toxics Coalition (near Oakland, California). By demonstrating, holding hearings and public workshops, conducting research, and filing suits against local and state governments, these groups have tried to draw attention to the racial and class biases that determine how hazardous waste sites are selected.

One of the pioneers of this environmental movement was Patsy Ruth Oliver, founder and leader of the Carver Terrace Community Action Group. When an investigation revealed that Carver Terrace, a black suburb outside of Texarkana, Texas, was built on an old toxic waste site and sold to unsuspecting black homebuyers, Texas officials asked that the federal government add it to its Superfund cleanup program (a $1.3 billion trust that Congress created to clean up toxic waste dumps). When the Environmental Protection Agency (EPA) came to investigate, it concluded that the soil was contaminated but that it posed no danger to the residents. Oliver and her neighbors were outraged, especially after they discovered that the EPA had withheld information suggesting that the residents were, in fact, at risk. Through persistence and protest, Oliver and the Community Action Group were able to force the government to buy them out and help them relocate. Although the people of Carver Terrace lost their homes, the buyout was a significant victory for the movement because they forced the government to acknowledge the seriousness of toxic dumping. Oliver continued to speak out against environmental racism until her death in 1993.

In the political arena, the 1990s for African Americans have truly been the best of times and the worst of times. Black gains in the electoral

Toxic waste dumps are far more likely to be located in or near poor minority communities than in more affluent, white ones.

sphere accompanied growing incidents of racism in public places; successful grassroots organizing followed discoveries of more toxic waste dumps; the spectacular rise of black women in national politics coincided with a vicious backlash against women in the society as a whole. And if this was not enough to complicate matters, the old order of black versus white was fast becoming obsolete. With the recent wave of immigration from nonwhite countries, African Americans found themselves surrounded by new neighbors, new cultures, and new issues with which they had to contend.

CHAPTER 8

BLACK TO THE FUTURE
IMMIGRATION AND THE NEW
REALITIES OF RACE

◇ ◇ ◇

While the decade of the 1990s was a period of resurgent black nationalism, it also was a period when what it meant to be "black" no longer was a simple matter. By the 1980s, the increase in black *immigrants* to the United States, most of whom came from the Caribbean, profoundly changed the cultural makeup of black communities.

Black immigration from the Caribbean did not begin in the 1980s; there had been vibrant West Indian communities, especially in New York City, at least as early as the 1920s. However, several factors contributed to the massive influx of West Indians to the United States in the late 20th century. First, the easing of restrictions on immigration to the United States after 1965 enabled greater numbers of West Indians to enter the country. Second, Britain imposed severe restrictions on immigrants from its own former colonies in 1962. Third, rising unemployment and poverty in the Caribbean during the 1970s and 1980s forced many West Indians to search for work in the United States. Thus, by the early 1980s approximately 50,000 legal immigrants from the English-speaking Caribbean and some 6,000 to 8,000 Haitians were entering the United States annually, about half of whom settled in New York City.

Despite myths of West Indian affluence and financial success as a result of thrift and hard work, the majority of immigrants were very poor and worked mainly in service sector jobs, such as janitors, cooks, secre-

Children take part in a "Kiddie Carnival" during New York City's 1990 West Indian Day parade.

121

taries, and clerical work. Some established independent businesses—
small groceries, taxi services, restaurants—but most of these are small,
family-run enterprises. Haitians have faced the most difficulties because
many are extremely poor refugees fleeing desperate poverty and political
violence. To make matters worse, during the administrations of Presidents Reagan and Bush many Haitian refugees were detained by the
Immigration and Naturalization Service and either deported or held in
camps or prisons until they received a hearing.

There have been tensions between these new black immigrants and
native-born African Americans, especially because they competed against
each other in a shrinking labor market. Even during the first wave of
immigration after World War I, most West Indians have been fiercely
independent in terms of maintaining their unique cultural heritage and
not identifying more generally with "black Americans." As their communities grew, West Indians became even more distinctive, creating
cultural institutions and political organizations that encouraged loyalty to
their home island, and carving out a separate niche for themselves in
black America.

On the whole, however, relations between West Indians and native-

Rastafarians were among the large number of West Indian immigrants coming into the United States during the 1980s. Because their religion forbids the cutting of hair, Rastafarians wear their hair in dreadlocks.

born African Americans have been good. Caribbean music, cuisine, and even dialects have been an integral part of African-American culture, especially on the East Coast. Many African Americans in New York City participate in Caribbean celebrations (especially "Carnival"), and West Indians have adopted a good deal of African-American popular culture. Caribbean youth were key contributors to the development of rap music.

The growth of Rastafarianism in the United States illustrates the impact black West Indian immigrants have had on African-American culture as a whole. Rastas, or members of the Rastafarian religious faith, regard the late Ethiopian emperor Haile Selassie as God. While preaching peace and love between the races, they also warn that some kind of race war is imminent. What made Rastafarianism appealing, aside from its highly spiritual form of black nationalism, was the culture surrounding it. Rastas tend to be vegetarians, do not drink alcohol, and wear their hair in dreadlocks. Their locks are never cut because hair is considered part of the spirit. The popularity of reggae music, in particular, was responsible for introducing Rastafarianism to American audiences. By 1990, there were about 1 million Rastas in the United States, at least 80,000 of whom resided in New York City.

Roy Innis, who was born in the Virgin Islands, participated in the civil rights movement of the 1960s. During the 1980s, however, Innis supported the conservative policies of President Reagan and was highly critical of liberal black leaders such as Jesse Jackson.

In the realm of politics, native-born African American and Caribbean communities have worked collectively to fight racism in New York City, and some West Indians have even risen to important leadership roles in traditional civil rights organizations. (The Congress on Racial Equality [CORE] has been headed by Virgin Islands native Roy Innis, although his Republican party affiliation has limited his political base among both West Indians and African Americans.) Similarly, African-American political leaders have maintained a longstanding interest in Caribbean politics. They have tended to support democratic political movements in the Caribbean and pushed for a more progressive U.S. policy toward that region. Some actively backed the struggle for independence from colonial rule back in the 1950s and 1960s.

As the number of Caribbean-born immigrants to the United States grows, what happens in the Caribbean takes on even greater importance in black politics. When President Reagan called for the invasion of the tiny island of Grenada in 1983, African Americans organized massive protests. Similarly, African-American political leaders have been among the most vocal supporters of Haitian refugees. After the democratically elected president of Haiti, Jean-Bertrand Aristide, was overthrown by the military and exiled in 1992, African Americans and West Indians consistently called for his return to power. Black political leaders have protested the Bush administration's harsh immigration policies toward Haiti, which often resulted in refusing entry to refugees fleeing political violence and starvation. Protests were also directed at the Clinton administration to develop a more active policy toward Haiti that would help restore democratic rule. As a result of demonstrations by several black members of Congress and a dramatic hunger strike waged by Randall Robinson, the president of a lobbying group called TransAfrica, President Clinton appointed former congressman Bill Gray as special envoy to Haiti. In October 1994, Clinton went even further, pressuring the Haitian military to relinquish power and dispatching U.S. troops to restore Aristide to the presidency.

America's changing cultural and ethnic landscape not only calls into question the longstanding (and always false) presumption that the country was divided into two races—black and white. It transformed the meaning of race relations in America's inner cities. Before 1965, Jews were probably the most visible ethnic group with whom urban blacks had contact who did not simply fall into the category of "white." Relations between blacks and Jews in the past had always been mixed, running the gamut from allies in radical organizations to economic competitors. Because some Jews owned small retail outlets in African-American communities—largely because anti-Semitism kept them from establishing businesses elsewhere—blacks and Jews sometimes dealt with each other on the basis of a consumer/proprietor relationship. In the aftermath of the urban riots of the late 1960s, however, most Jewish merchants sold off their businesses and the few still residing in the ghetto moved out. Except for places like Brooklyn's Crown Heights community, where tensions between blacks (mostly West Indians) and Hasidic Jews erupted in a major riot in 1991, few inner city blacks live in close proximity to Jews.

After the U.S. invasion of the island of Grenada in 1983, many African Americans joined in protests denouncing the action.

But as the Jews moved out of the inner city, new groups of immigrants moved in. The most prominent of the post-1965 wave of immigrants settling in or near African-American communities were Asians from Korea, Vietnam, Cambodia, the Philippines and Samoa, and Latinos from Central America, Cuba, Mexico, and the Dominican Republic. The combination of economic competition, declining opportunities, scarce public resources, and racist attitudes led to a marked increase in interethnic conflict. In South Central Los Angeles, once an all-black community, Latinos made up about one-fourth of the population in 1992. Job and housing competition between Latinos (most of whom are Central American and Mexican immigrants) and African Americans created enormous tensions between these two groups. Black residents, who in the past had been indifferent to immigration, began supporting measures to limit the entry of Latinos into the United States.

On the other hand, Koreans have been singled out by both blacks and Latinos because a handful own retail establishments and rental property in the poorer sections of South Central Los Angeles. African-American and Latino residents believed the federal government favored Korean immigrants by offering them low interest loans and grants. The fact is, however, that few Korean merchants received federal aid. The majority in Los Angeles and elsewhere ran small family businesses—mainly liquor stores, groceries, discount markets, and specialized shops such as hair care and manicure supply outlets. Often investing what little capital they brought with them from their home country, Koreans relied on family labor and maintained businesses with very low profit margins. Moreover, the idea that Koreans were denying blacks the opportunity to "own their own" businesses ignores the fact that most Korean establishments (particularly liquor stores) were purchased at enormously high prices from African Americans, who in turn had bought these businesses at high prices from Jews fleeing South Central in the late 1960s and early 1970s.

Last, and perhaps most important, the vast majority of Koreans were neither merchants nor landlords; they were low-wage workers. Nevertheless, blacks and Latinos perceived Koreans as thriving newcomers, backed by a white racist government, taking money and opportunities away from the residents. These perceptions were intensified by the myth that all Asian immigrants were "model minorities," hard-working and successful entrepreneurs who settled comfortably in the United States, and by a general anti-Asian sentiment that had swept the country after the recessions of the 1970s and 1980s.

But these interethnic tensions were not based entirely on myths. The daily interactions between blacks and Latinos and Korean merchants generated enormous hostility. A common complaint in Los Angeles and elsewhere (most notably, New York) was that Korean merchants treated black and Latino consumers disrespectfully. Fearful of crime, some Korean store owners have been known to follow customers down the aisles, ask to inspect customers' handbags, and refuse entry to young black males who they think looked "suspicious."

By the early 1990s, tensions between African Americans and Korean merchants escalated to the point of violence. In one six-month period in 1991, at least three African Americans and two Koreans were killed as a result of customer/proprietor disputes. The most dramatic

A black man shops at a Korean-owned grocery store in Brooklyn, New York. In many cities, tensions run high between blacks and Korean merchants.

encounter was the fatal shooting of 15-year-old Latasha Harlins in Los Angeles by Korean grocer Soon Ja Du, which was captured on videotape and played on network news programs throughout the country. The incident began when Du accused Harlins of stealing a $1.79 bottle of orange juice in spite of the fact that she held the bottle in clear view and had not attempted to leave the store. Angered by the accusation, Harlins exchanged harsh words with Du, and they engaged in some mutual shoving. As soon as Harlins struck a final blow and began to walk out of the store, Soon Ja Du pulled out a pistol from behind the counter and shot her in the back of the head.

African Americans were shocked and saddened by the shooting. Harlins's family pointed out that Latasha was an honor student at Compton High School and had no history of trouble. Local organizations called for boycotts of Korean-owned businesses, and tensions between merchants and community residents escalated even further. But black anger over the shooting turned to outrage when Judge Joyce Karlin sentenced Du to five years probation, a $500 fine, and community service, prompting a long-uttered lament among African Americans that a black person's life was of minimal value in the United States. Insult was added to injury when, five days after Du's sentencing, a black man from nearby Glendale, California, had to serve 30 days in jail for beating his dog.

Tragically, the Soon Ja Du case and the media coverage of it not only contributed to the myth that African Americans are criminals, but ultimately reinforced dominant stereotypes about Korean immigrants too. By giving Du probation and community service, the judge sent the message that the killing of Harlins was partially justifiable because Du viewed her as a potentially violent criminal. Thus the actual roles in the case were reversed by the judge's ruling: Du became the victim and Harlins the perpetrator. Moreover, by characterizing the incident as a black/Korean conflict rather than the actions of a single merchant, both the media and black community activists portrayed Soon Ja Du as representative of *all* Korean merchants. Rather than focus the boycott on her store, blacks targeted all Korean-owned stores.

This combination of interethnic tensions, white racism, and immense poverty exploded on April 29, 1992, when Los Angeles experienced the most widespread and devastating urban uprising in the history of the United States. The spark for the rebellion was a police brutality trial that ended in the acquittal of four officers who had savagely beaten a black motorist named Rodney King 13 months earlier. Unlike most incidents of police brutality, this one was captured on videotape by George Holliday, a white plumbing company manager. Holliday tried to report the incident to Los Angeles Police Department officials, but he was rebuffed. Instead, he sold the videotape to a local television station and it soon became national news. The entire nation watched King writhe in pain as he absorbed 56 blows in a span of 81 seconds. In addition to punching, kicking, and whacking King with a wooden baton, police shocked him twice with a high voltage stun gun. When it was all over, King was left with a broken cheekbone, nine skull fractures, a shattered eye socket, and a broken ankle and needed 20 stitches in his face.

For most viewers, regardless of race, the videotape proved beyond a shadow of a doubt that the officers involved in the beating used

On April 29, 1992, riots erupted in Los Angeles after an all-white jury acquitted four Los Angeles police officers of beating a black man named Rodney King. On May 1, King spoke to reporters and called for an end to the violence.

excessive force. Thus, when the all-white jury handed down a not-guilty verdict on April 29, 1992, African Americans were shocked, saddened, and then very angry. Throughout Los Angeles, from South Central to downtown, groups of black people began to vent their rage. They were soon joined by Latinos and whites who were also shocked by the verdict. But as the violence unfolded, it became very clear that these riots were not just about the injustice meted out to Rodney King. As one black L.A. resident explained, "It wasn't just the Rodney King verdict. It's the whole thing, the shooting of Latasha Harlins and the lack of jail time for that Korean woman." In some neighborhoods, therefore, blacks and Latinos attacked Korean-owned businesses, white motorists, and each other rather than the police. Among the biggest targets were liquor stores, long seen as the cause of many of the black community's woes. And in the midst of chaos, virtually everyone went after property, seizing furniture, appliances, clothes, and most of all, food.

Unlike previous "race riots," the events in Los Angeles were multiethnic and not limited to the predominantly black ghettoes. Buildings burned from West Los Angeles and Watts to Koreatown, Long Beach, and Santa Monica. Of the first 5,000 people arrested, 52 percent were Latino and only 39 percent were African American. When the smoke finally began to clear on May 2, at least 58 people were killed (26 African Americans, 18 Latinos, 10 whites, 2 Asians, 2 unknown) and thousands were injured. The fires left more than 5,000 buildings destroyed or badly damaged. The estimated property damage totaled a staggering $785 million.

More than any other event, the L.A. uprising dramatized to the rest of the country the tragic plight of urban America. And because it occurred during a Presidential election year, there was enormous pressure on President George Bush to offer a prompt response. He proposed Operation Weed and Seed, an urban policy that would provide big tax breaks to entrepreneurs willing to invest in inner cities, some limited programs for disadvantaged children, and a massive buildup of the police and criminal justice system. Indeed, the real emphasis was on the "weed" rather than the "seed" component; nearly 80 percent of the proposed $500 million allocation was earmarked for policing. Bush's proposals were severely criticized by liberal black political leaders and scholars. They felt that the "law-and-order" emphasis was misplaced and that giving tax breaks to companies was not enough to attract capital to South

Central L.A. Attempts to do the same thing in the past have failed. On the other hand, black elected officials responded to the rebellion by holding meetings and conferences, and by visiting communities damaged by the riots. Established black leaders criticized the Bush administration's proposals but few proposed policies of their own. One exception was Representative Maxine Waters, who tried desperately but failed to get Congress to pass a sweeping and much-needed urban aid bill.

Ironically, one of the clearest and most comprehensive proposals came from leaders of the two largest black street gangs in Los Angeles. After a long and violent rivalry, leaders of the Bloods and the Crips called a truce and drafted a document called "Give Us the Hammer and the Nails and We Will Rebuild the City." The proposal asked for $2 billion to rebuild deteriorating and damaged neighborhoods; $1 billion to establish hospitals and health-care clinics to South Central Los Angeles; $700 million to improve public education and refurbish schools; $20 million in low-interest loans for minority businesses; $6 million to fund a new law enforcement program that would allow ex-gang members, with

Los Angeles residents work together to clean up the debris from the devastating riots that tore the city apart. Fifty-eight people were killed, thousands more were injured, and the estimated damage to property was $785 million.

A few days after the riots ended in Los Angeles, members of several rival gangs called a press conference to announce a truce.

the proper training, to accompany the LAPD patrols of the community. If these demands were met, the authors promised to rid Los Angeles of drug dealers and provide matching funds for an AIDS research and awareness center. Of course, some of these same gangs were involved in the drug trade themselves, suggesting that their proposal would eliminate an important source of their own revenue. Besides, it is doubtful that the Bloods and the Crips could raise matching funds. In any event, their efforts were to no avail; the mayor and the city council completely ignored the gang members' proposal.

Despite a deluge of plans and proposals, black Los Angeles remained pretty much unchanged in 1994. Two years after the riots, unemployment was still sky high, job opportunities were scarce, and the historic truce between the Crips and the Bloods had begun to unravel locally. Nevertheless, what happened in Los Angeles represented a kind of crossroads for the United States. It vividly called into question the idea that race relations in this country can be viewed as "black and white." It also underscored the extent of desperation in cities generated

131

by the new global economy. The days when jobs were plentiful, even if they were low-wage jobs, are gone. Now America's inner city has an army of permanently unemployed men and women who have little or no hope of living the American Dream. Most keep pushing on. A handful turn to the underground, the illegal economy of bartering stolen goods and drugs. In some neighborhoods, that is all that is left. Meanwhile, the police deal with this tragedy by placing virtually every black person under siege.

And yet, on the outskirts of these crumbling ghettos are black folk who live the American dream. Though they, too, have their share of nightmares, of racist humiliation, of invisible barriers, even of violence, they are a little safer, a little more secure, and a lot richer. At moments they are as distant from ghetto residents as white farmers in Iowa. At other times they are as close as kin. In a strange way, the L.A. rebellion simultaneously brought them together and tore them apart. It brought them together because they shared the experience of racial humiliation, of realizing that black life, no matter how much money one has, is valued less than white life. It tore them apart because it underscored the growing chasm dividing rich and poor.

AFTERWORD

◇ ◇ ◇

The generation that came of age in the '70s, '80s, and '90s has been called a lot of things: the post-soul generation, the post–civil rights generation, the postindustrial generation. But few standing "at the edge of history," to use the language of the Gary Declaration, thought in terms of being "post" anything. Rather, they entered a new period with tremendous optimism. For some, this sense of a better future came because of efforts toward racial integration. For others it was the hope for greater political and social control of their lives. For most African Americans it was a combination of both with a little fun and pleasure thrown in for good measure.

Few anticipated the economic, social, and political crises poor urban blacks would have to face, and fewer still imagined the plush black suburbs of Prince Georges County, Maryland, or that several black-owned companies might one day dwarf Motown Records. Although each difficult day questioned their faith in this country, young mothers and fathers hoped that racism would diminish a little and life for their children would be much easier. In some cases their lives *were* much easier; in other cases a racist police officer's bullet or the fists, sticks, and stones of skinheads cut their young lives short. The sad reality, however, is that the most likely source of death for a young, healthy black man is a gunshot from another black man.

But this story is not finished yet, and it need not have a tragic ending. The chapters to come will be written by all of us still living, including you who hold this book in your hands. What we add to this story as we step into the 21st century depends, to a large degree, on us . . . all of us: black and white, Latino and Asian, Native American and Arab American, Jew and Gentile, women and men, rich and poor. If there is one thing we have learned from this book, and from all 11 volumes in this series, it is that the problems facing African Americans are not simply outgrowths of a crisis in *black* America. They are products of America's crisis. We must constantly remind ourselves that America's future is bound up with the descendants of slaves and the circumstances they must endure. As police brutality victim Rodney King put it in his memorable press conference following the Los Angeles uprising, "We're all stuck here for a while."

Chronology

1970

Kenneth Gibson becomes Newark, New Jersey's first black mayor.

1970

Race riots erupt in several cities, including Philadelphia; New Orleans; New Bedford, Massachusetts; and Hartford, Connecticut.

SEPTEMBER 1970

Black Panther party, along with women's and gay liberation activists, holds the Revolutionary People's Constitutional Convention in Philadelphia.

OCTOBER 13, 1970

Angela Davis arrested, and charged with murder, kidnapping, and conspiracy; case prompts an international campaign to free her. Two years later, she is found not guilty.

1971

Congressional Black Caucus is founded.

1972

Shirley Chisholm becomes first African American in history to seek the Democratic party's Presidential nomination.

1972

Coalition of Black Trade Unionists is founded.

MARCH 1972

National Black Political Assembly holds its founding convention in Gary, Indiana.

1973

National Black Feminist Organization is founded.

1973

Tom Bradley elected first black mayor of Los Angeles.

1973–75

United States experiences worst economic recession in decades.

1974

President Richard M. Nixon resigns after his administration is implicated in the Watergate scandal. Gerald Ford is sworn in as President.

1975

NAACP wins court order to integrate Boston schools by busing black children from Roxbury to predominantly white schools in Charlestown. Transition marred by violence.

1975

Wallace D. Muhammad takes over Nation of Islam after death of his father, Elijah Muhammad. He denounces his father's teachings, adopts orthodox Islam, and changes the name of the organization to the World Community of al-Islam in the West.

1976

Democrat Jimmy Carter elected President.

FEBRUARY 1977

Television miniseries "Roots," based on Alex Haley's best-selling novel, is watched by a record 130 million viewers, sparking a national debate about race and African-American history.

1978

Black unemployment rate nearly 2.5 times higher than white; largest gap since the federal government began keeping such statistics.

1978

Allan Bakke's successful suit against University of California, Davis, Medical School charging "reverse discrimination" weakens affirmative action policies. Supreme Court rules in *Regents of the University of California* v. *Bakke* (1978) that Bakke had been denied "equal protection of the laws" as required by the 14th Amendment.

1978

Louis Farrakhan breaks with Wallace D. Muhammad and reestablishes the Nation of Islam under Elijah Muhammad's original beliefs.

1979

The Sugar Hill Gang releases the first commercially successful rap single.

1980

Republican Ronald Reagan is elected President.

MAY 1980

African Americans in Liberty City, Florida, riot after police officers are acquitted for killing an unarmed black man.

NOVEMBER 1980

National Black Independent Political party is founded.

1982

Alice Walker publishes *The Color Purple,* which received the American Book Award and the Pulitzer Prize. Three years later it is turned into a highly successful feature film.

1982

Struggle to block a toxic waste dump in Warren County, North Carolina, launches a national movement against environmental racism.

1983

Harold Washington is elected first black mayor of Chicago.

1984

Jesse Jackson makes first bid for the Democratic party's Presidential nomina-

tion, receiving about 3.5 million popular votes in the primaries.

1984

"The Cosby Show" makes its debut, becoming the most popular regular program on television.

MAY 1985

Black Philadelphia mayor Wilson Goode directs the police to bomb the headquarters of MOVE, a local black nationalist organization. The bombing leaves 11 people dead and 250 people homeless.

SEPTEMBER 1985

U.S. Census Bureau reports that one out of three African Americans is living below the poverty line.

1986

Spike Lee releases his highly successful first feature film, *She's Gotta Have It,* igniting Hollywood's interest in young black male filmmakers.

1988

Jesse Jackson seeks Democratic Presiden-

tial nomination for a second time. Receives 7 million votes and is Michael Dukakis's strongest challenger for the nomination.

1988

The Black Women Mayor's Caucus is founded.

1989

Douglas L. Wilder is elected governor of Virginia; he becomes the first African American elected governor of any state.

1990

Sharon Pratt Kelly (formerly Dixon) is elected mayor of Washington, D.C. She is the first African American and first native of the district to hold that post.

1991

Julie Dash releases *Daughters of the Dust,* the first feature film by an African-American woman.

OCTOBER 1991

Anita Hill's testimony during the confirmation hearings of Supreme Court Justice

Clarence Thomas launches a nationwide discussion of sexual harassment.

1992

Carol Moseley-Braun becomes first African American woman elected to the U.S. Senate.

APRIL 29-MAY 1, 1992

Acquittal of four Los Angeles police officers accused of using excessive force on black motorist Rodney King sparks the largest, most costly urban rebellion in U.S. history.

1993

Novelist Toni Morrison wins Nobel Prize for literature.

MAY 1994

Class-action suit forces Denny's restaurant chain to pay $54 million in damages for systematically discriminating against African-American customers.

FURTHER READING

GENERAL AFRICAN-AMERICAN HISTORY

Bennett, Lerone, Jr. *Before the Mayflower: A History of Black America.* 6th rev. ed. New York: Viking Penguin, 1988.

———. *The Shaping of Black America.* New York: Viking Penguin, 1993.

Berry, Mary Frances, and John W. Blassingame. *Long Memory: The Black Experience in America.* New York: Oxford University Press, 1982.

Foner, Philip S. *History of Black Americans: From Africa to the Emergence of the Cotton Kingdom.* Westport, Conn.: Greenwood, 1975.

Franklin, John Hope, and August Meier. *Black Leaders of the 20th Century.* Urbana: University of Illinois Press, 1982.

Franklin, John Hope, and Alfred A. Moss, Jr. *From Slavery to Freedom: A History of African Americans.* 7th ed. New York: Knopf, 1994.

Garwood, Alfred N., comp., *Black Americans: A Statistical Sourcebook 1992.* Boulder, Colo.: Numbers and Concepts, 1993.

Gates, Henry L., Jr. *A Chronology of African-American History from 1445–1980.* New York: Amistad, 1980.

Giddings, Paula. *When and Where I Enter: The Impact of Black Women on Race and Sex in America.* New York: Bantam, 1985.

Harding, Vincent. *There is a River: The Black Struggle for Freedom in America.* San Diego: Harcourt Brace, 1981.

Harris, William H. *The Harder We Run: Black Workers Since the Civil War.* New York: Oxford University Press, 1982.

Hine, Darlene C., et al., eds. *Black Women in America.* Brooklyn, N.Y.: Carlson, 1993.

Jaynes, Gerald David, and Robin M. Williams, Jr., *A Common Destiny: Blacks and American Society.* Washington, D.C.: National Academy Press, 1989.

Jones, Jacqueline. *Labor of Love, Labor of Sorrow: Black Women, Work, and the Family from Slavery to the Present.* New York: Vintage, 1986.

Medearis, Angela Shelf. *Come This Far to Freedom: A History of African Americans.* New York: Atheneum, 1993.

Meltzer, Milton. *The Black Americans: A History in Their Own Words.* Rev. ed. New York: HarperCollins, 1984.

Mintz, Sidney W., and Richard Price. *The Birth of African-American Culture: An Anthropological Perspective.* Boston: Beacon Press, 1992.

Quarles, Benjamin. *The Negro in the Making of America.* 3rd ed. New York: Macmillan, 1987.

GENERAL HISTORIES OF THE UNITED STATES

Amott, Teresa L., and Julie A. Matthaei. *Race, Gender, and Work: A Multicultural History of Women in the United States.* Boston: South End Press, 1991.

Carroll, Peter N. *It Seemed Like Nothing Happened: The Tragedy and Promise of America in the 1970s.* New York: Holt, Rinehart and Winston, 1982.

Coontz, Stephanie. *The Way We Never Were: American Families and the Nostalgia Trap.* New York: Basic Books, 1992.

Edsall, Thomas Byrne. *Chain Reaction: The Impact of Race, Rights, and Taxes on American Politics.* New York: Norton, 1991.

Evans, Sara M. *Born for Liberty: A History of Women in America.* New York: Free Press, 1989.

Piven, Frances Fox. *The New Class War: Reagan's Attack on the Welfare State and its Consequences.* New York: Pantheon, 1982.

Siegel, Frederick F. *Troubled Journey: From Pearl Harbor to Ronald Reagan.* New York: Hill and Wang, 1984.

Stacey, Judith. *Brave New Families: Stories of Domestic Upheaval in Late Twentieth Century America*. New York: Basic Books, 1990.

AFRICAN-AMERICAN POLITICS

Bell, Derrick. *And We Are Not Saved: The Elusive Quest for Racial Justice*. New York: Basic Books, 1987.

Collins, Sheila D. *The Rainbow Challenge: The Jackson Campaign and the Future of U.S. Politics*. New York: Monthly Review Press, 1986.

Davis, Angela. *Women, Culture, and Politics*. New York: Random House, 1989.

Harding, Vincent. *Hope and History: Why We Must Share the Story of the Movement*. Maryknoll, N.Y.: Orbis, 1990.

Hatch, Roger D., and Frank E. Watkins, eds. *Reverend Jesse L. Jackson: Straight from the Heart*. Philadelphia: Fortress Press, 1987.

Henry, Charles. *Jesse Jackson: The Search for Common Ground*. Oakland: Black Scholar Press, 1991.

Lawson, Steven F. *Running for Freedom: Civil Rights and Black Politics in America Since 1941*. Philadelphia: Temple University Press, 1991.

Lusane, Clarence. *African Americans at the Crossroads: The Restructuring of Black Leadership in the 1992 Elections*. Boston: South End Press, 1994.

Marable, Manning. *Race, Reform, and Rebellion: The Second Reconstruction in Black America, 1945–1990*. 2nd ed. Jackson: University Press of Mississippi, 1991.

McKissack, Patricia, and Frederick McKissack. *The Civil Rights Movement in America from 1865 to the Present*. Chicago: Children's Press, 1987.

Morrison, Toni, ed. *Race-ing Justice, En-gendering Power: Essays on Anita Hill, Clarence Thomas and the Construction of Social Reality*. New York: Pantheon, 1992.

Myers, Walter Dean. *Now Is Your Time: The African-American Struggle for Freedom*. New York: HarperCollins, 1991.

West, Cornel. *Race Matters*. Boston: Beacon Press, 1993.

AFRICAN-AMERICAN SOCIAL AND ECONOMIC CONDITIONS

Banner-Haley, Charles T. *The Fruits of Integration: Black Middle-Class Ideology and Culture, 1960–1990*. Jackson: University Press of Mississippi, 1994.

Billingsley, Andrew. *Climbing Jacob's Ladder: The Enduring Legacy of African-American Families*. New York: Simon & Schuster, 1992.

Davis, Mike. *City of Quartz: Excavating the Future in Los Angeles*. London: Verso Books, 1990.

Feagin, Joe R., and Melvin P. Sikes. *Living with Racism: The Black Middle-Class Experience*. Boston: Beacon Press, 1994.

Gill, Gerald. *Meanness Mania: The Changed Mood*. Washington, D.C.: Howard University Press, 1980.

Glasgow, Douglas G. *The Black Underclass: Poverty, Unemployment, and Entrapment of Ghetto Youth*. New York: Vintage, 1981.

Jones, Jacqueline. *The Dispossessed: America's Underclasses from the Civil War to the Present*. New York: Basic Books, 1992.

Kasinitz, Philip. *Caribbean New York: Black Immigrants and the Politics of Race*. Ithaca, N.Y.: Cornell University Press, 1992.

Landry, Bart. *The New Black Middle Class*. Berkeley: University of California Press, 1987.

Lusane, Clarence. *Pipe Dream Blues: Racism and the War on Drugs*. Boston: South End Press, 1991.

Madhubuti, Haki R., ed. *Why L.A. Happened: Implications of the '92 Los Angeles Rebellion.* Chicago: Third World Press, 1993.

Rank, Mark Robert. *Living on the Edge: The Realities of Welfare in America.* New York: Columbia University Press, 1994.

Simms, Margaret C., and Julianne Malveaux, eds. *Slipping Through the Cracks: The Status of Black Women.* New Brunswick, N.J.: Transaction Books, 1986.

Wilson, William J. *The Truly Disadvantaged: The Inner City, the Underclass, and Public Policy.* Chicago: University of Chicago Press, 1987.

AFRICAN-AMERICAN CULTURE

Castleman, Craig. *Getting Up: Subway Graffiti in New York.* Cambridge, Mass.: MIT Press, 1982.

Cross, Brian. *It's Not About a Salary . . . Rap, Race and Resistance in Los Angeles.* London: Verso Books, 1993.

Dates, Jannette L., and William Barlow, eds. *Split Image: African Americans in the Mass Media.* 2nd ed. Washington, D.C.: Howard University Press, 1993.

Dent, Gina, ed. *Black Popular Culture.* Seattle: Bay Press, 1992.

George, Nelson. *The Death of Rhythm and Blues.* New York: Plume, 1988.

Guerrero, Ed. *Framing Blackness: The African-American Image in Film.* Philadelphia: Temple University Press, 1993.

Hazzard-Gordon, Katrina. *Jookin': The Rise of Social Dance Formations in African-American Culture.* Philadelphia: Temple University Press, 1990.

Lippard, Lucy R. *Mixed Blessings: New Art in a Multicultural America.* New York: Pantheon, 1990.

MacDonald, J. Fred. *Blacks and White TV: Afro-Americans in Television since 1948.* Chicago: Nelson-Hall, 1983.

Rose, Tricia. *Black Noise: Rap Music and Black Culture in Contemporary America.* Middletown, Conn.: Wesleyan University Press, 1994.

Tate, Greg. *Flyboy in the Buttermilk: Essays on Contemporary America.* New York: Simon & Schuster, 1992.

Van Deburg, William L. *New Day in Babylon: The Black Power Movement and American Culture, 1965–1975.* Chicago: University of Chicago Press, 1992.

MEMOIRS, BIOGRAPHIES, AUTOBIOGRAPHIES, ORAL HISTORIES

Bernotas, Bob. *Amiri Baraka.* New York: Chelsea House, 1991.

Carter, Stephen L. *Reflections of an Affirmative Action Baby.* New York: Basic Books, 1991.

Chisholm, Shirley. *The Good Fight.* New York: Harper & Row, 1973.

Delany, Samuel R. *The Motion of Light in Water.* New York: William Morrow, 1988.

Gwaltney, John Langston. *Drylongso: A Self-Portrait of Black America.* New York: Vintage, 1981.

Herbert, Solomon J., and George H. Hill. *Bill Cosby.* New York: Chelsea House, 1991.

Lanker, Brian. *I Dream a World: Portraits of Black Women Who Changed America.* New York: Stewart, Tabori, and Chang, 1989.

Lewis, Reginald, and Blair S. Walker. *Why Should White Guys Have all the Fun?* New York: Wiley, 1995.

McCall, Nathan. *Makes Me Wanna Holler: A Young Black Man in America.* New York: Random House, 1994.

Shakur, Sanyika ["Monster" Kody Scott]. *Monster: The Autobiography of an L.A. Gang Member*. New York: Penguin, 1993.

Tarpley, Natasha, ed. *Testimony: Young African Americans on Self-Discovery and Black Identity*. Boston: Beacon Press, 1994.

Terkel, Studs. *Race: How Blacks and Whites Think and Feel About the American Obsession*. New York: New Press, 1992.

Thomas, Arthur E. *Like It Is: Arthur E. Thomas Interviews Leaders on Black America*. Edited by Emily Rovetch. New York: Dutton, 1981.

Williams, Patricia. *The Alchemy of Race and Rights: Diary of a Law Professor*. Cambridge, Mass.: Harvard University Press, 1991.

FICTION

Butler, Octavia E. *Imago*. New York: Warner Books, 1989.

Danticat, Edwidge. *Breath, Eyes, Memory: A Novel*. New York: Soho Press, 1994.

Delany, Samuel R. *Dahlgren*. New York: Bantam, 1975.

Guy, Rosa. *And I Heard a Bird Sing*. New York: Delacorte Press, 1987.

———. *New Guys Around the Block*. London: Gollancz, 1983.

Morrison, Toni. *Beloved*. New York: Random House, 1987.

———. *Jazz*. New York: Random House, 1992.

Mosley, Walter. *Devil in a Blue Dress*. New York: Norton, 1990.

Mowry, Jess. *Way Past Cool*. New York: Farrar, Strauss, and Giroux, 1992.

Shange, Ntozake. *For Colored Girls Who Have Considered Suicide, When the Rainbow is Enuf: A Choreopoem*. New York: Bantam, 1980.

———. *Sassafrass, Cypress & Indigo*. New York: St. Martin's, 1982.

Walker, Alice. *The Color Purple*. New York: Harcourt Brace, 1982.

Woodson, Jacqueline. *Between Madison & Palmetto*. New York: Delacorte, 1993.

INDEX

◇ ◇ ◇

ACKNOWLEDGMENTS

◇ ◇ ◇

I would like to extend a special thanks to Diedra Harris-Kelley for her love, support, and insights into post-1970 African-American culture and to Earl Lewis for his critical eye and unwavering encouragement. I am also deeply grateful to Elsa Barkley Brown, David Freund, Clarence Lusane, Marya McQuirter, Tricia Rose, James Spady, and Makani Themba for suggestions and corrections they made along the way. To the many, many kids I spoke with in schools, detention centers, prisons, and youth centers who continued to remind me what the current generation of youth is up against, my gratitude runs deep. Finally, thanks to my beautiful daughter Elleza. Although she's just learning to read as this book goes to press, our discussions have been invaluable nonetheless.

PICTURE CREDITS

◇ ◇ ◇

ROBIN D. G. KELLEY

◇ ◇ ◇

Robin D. G. Kelley is professor of history and Africana studies at New York University. He previously taught history and African-American studies at the University of Michigan. He is the author of *Hammer and Hoe: Alabama Communists during the Great Depression*, which received the Eliot Rudwick Prize of the Organization of American Historians and was named Outstanding Book on Human Rights by the Gustavus Myers Center for the Study of Human Rights in the United States. Professor Kelley is also the author of *Race Rebels: Culture, Politics, and the Black Working Class* and co-editor of *Imagining Home: Class, Culture, and Nationalism in the African Diaspora.*

EARL LEWIS

◇ ◇ ◇

Earl Lewis is professor of history and Afroamerican studies at the University of Michigan. He served as director of the university's Center for Afroamerican and African Studies from 1990 to 1993. Professor Lewis is the author of *In Their Own Interests: Race, Class and Power in Twentieth Century Norfolk* and co-author of *Blacks in the Industrial Age: A Documentary History.*